Praise

What Leaders Are Saying

"Pitima's principles are simple and easy to implement, but the results you will achieve will be even more extraordinary than you could ever imagine. The impossible becomes possible when you apply the strategies in this magnificent book."

Gregory H. Johnson
NASA Astronaut, 2 Space Missions, Texas

"A map to guide people with the lantern of intelligence to a better personal, family and professional future."

Tony Buzan
Inventor of Mind Mapping, UK

"Pitima's journey from the penniless streets of Bangkok to mixing with the upper echelons of society offers a story of hope for millions looking to improve the quality of their lives. In a compelling, profound and systematic way she lays out a series of steps, thought processes, insights and action points that can only come from someone who has been there and got the results."

Peter Sage
Founder of the Million Dollar Secret Series, Dubai

"Pitima is best in class in the realm of human behaviour, personal development and peak performance. She can remarkably unleash your full potential, show hidden resources and guide you to achieve your biggest dreams. *Unstoppable You™* is a detailed guide to creating the life that you desire and deserve. Read this book in its entirety, apply what you learn and experience your life transforming into a masterpiece filled with an abundance of success and happiness. I know you will experience the best life has to offer."

Raymond Aaron
New York Times Bestselling Author, Canada

"If you thought you knew everything about how to be successful in life and business, wait until you read what is inside *Unstoppable You™*. From an employee to the world's most successful CEO, this book teaches you how to create even more success and happiness in your life."

Bill Walsh
Founder of Powerteam International, Chicago

"Pitima is one of the top peak performance strategists. The success principles in this influential book are worth remembering and applying for a life time. *Unstoppable You™* empowers you to create immediate and lasting results in all areas of your life."

Ron White
Two Time USA Memory Champion, Texas

"*Unstoppable You™* is one of the greatest gifts that you can treat yourself to. It has made a remarkable difference in my life. It brought out the best in me and showed me new opportunities that I did not know existed. I am unstoppable!"

Chalermkiat Suntipongpiboon
Squadron Leader, Air Force, Bangkok

"*Unstoppable You™* is a must-read book for success and happiness seekers. The fundamentals of all the success and happiness you ever wanted are revealed in this book. When you follow the step-by-step systems in this influential book, you are unstoppable."

Vincent Wong
Co-Founder of Wealth Dragons, UK

"Pitima provides straightforward steps to clarify your goals and make your dreams achievable. *Unstoppable You™* is an essential book to skyrocket your success."

Dan Forster
Executive Director, Investment Bank, London

To See the Complete Praise,
Visit
www.BeTheUnstoppableYou.com/Praise

Unstoppable You™

11 Strategies for Living Your Biggest Dreams

First published in Great Britain in 2015
by the Raymond Aaron Group

Copyright © Pitima Tongme 2015

Pitima Tongme has asserted her right under the Copyright, Design and Patents Act 1988 to be identified as the author of this work.

ISBN 1928155588

All rights reserved. No part of this publication may be reproduced, stored in a retrieval system, or transmitted, in any form or by any means, electronic, mechanical, photocopying, recording or otherwise, without the prior written permission of the author except in the case of brief quotations embodied in critical articles and reviews.

This book is sold subject to the condition that it shall not, by way of trade or otherwise, be lent, resold, hired out, or otherwise circulated without the author's prior consent in any form of binding or cover other than that in which it is published and without a similar condition, including this condition, being imposed on the subsequent purchaser.

Also By Pitima Tongme

Breakthrough to Success™

Coaching with Pitima Tongme:

Private VIP Coaching

Event with Pitima Tongme:

Success Academy™
Corporate Training
Keynote Speaking

Meet Pitima online and receive free £250 gifts at
www.BeTheUnstoppableYou.com/BookVIP

Unstoppable You™

*11 Strategies for Living
Your Biggest Dreams*

This book is being given to

_____

because I care about you and your greater success,

PITIMA TONGME

Connect with our success community
Facebook: www.facebook.com/UnstoppableYou
Youtube: www.youtube.com/PitimaTongme
Twitter: www.twitter.com/PitimaTongme

Table of Contents

Forewords		xv
Acknowledgements		xxii
Introduction		xxvii

Chapter 1: Victor of Your Destiny — 3
7 Strategies to Escape the Wheel of Your Demons

Chapter 2: Remarkable Breakthrough — 25
3 Strategies to Awaken the Hero within You

Chapter 3: Irresistible Life Design — 41
3 Powerful Models that Direct Your Future

Chapter 4: Instant State Transformation — 71
3 Techniques to Change Your State in a Heartbeat

Chapter 5: Essential Actions — 85
5 Steps to Turn Your Dreams into Your Reality

Chapter 6:	**Legendary Mastermind**	**121**
	How to Win and Influence Almost Anyone	
Chapter 7:	**Advanced Affirmation**	**155**
	5 Steps to Summon the Best You	
Chapter 8:	**Miraculous Visualisation**	**163**
	Seeing What You Want and Getting What You See	
Chapter 9:	**Ultimate Rehearsal**	**179**
	The Psychology of Living Your Dreams Now	
Chapter 10:	**Alluring Law of Attraction**	**185**
	How to Effortlessly Attract What Your Heart Desires	
Chapter 11:	**Breathtaking View of Your World**	**201**
	2 Models for the Happiest You	
Special	**My Story**	**226**
	You Can Change the World	**235**
	Your VIP Bonus	**237**
	Your Success Journey	**241**
	About the Author	**245**

The Power of Dream™

- The Art of Fulfillment
- The Psychology of Accelerating
- The Formula of Achievement
- The Power of Freedom

Unstoppable You™ is organised into 4 sections.

Section 1: The Power of Freedom provides powerful strategies to defeat your demons (Fear, Procrastination and Limited Belief) once and for all and awaken the hero that can conquer all challenges. All you need is within you. Your belief is the root cause of your failure or success. When you have absolute certainty that you can accomplish anything, you achieve more in life. This truth empowers you to amplify your vision and makes you become even more invincible in Section 2.

Section 2: The Formula of Achievement is: Vision -> State -> Action = Result. You get the result you want when you know what you want, be in the state that empowers you to get it and take massive determined actions until you accomplish it. You accomplish your goals faster by modelling success.

Section 3: The Psychology of Accelerating reveals additonal strategies that empower you to accelerate the achievement of your goals in a more enjoyable way. These powerful secrets are used by great innovators, top entrepreneurs, world champions and award winning celebrities throughout history.

Section 4: The Art of Fulfillment adjusts your model of the world so that you feel even more fulfilled and achieve greater success. You are going to discover the principles, which the happiest people live by, and become happier forever and ever.

The Power of Freedom

Chapter 1: **7 Strategies to Escape the Wheel of Your Demons**

Potential Results[x]   You confront your demons and conquer them once and for all. Fear, Procrastination and Limited Belief no longer stop you from getting what your heart desires.

Chapter 2: **3 Strategies to Awaken the Hero within You**

Potential Results[x]   You unleash more resources in a more powerful way, that you did not think was possible. You awaken the greatest warrior within you to help you overcome any challenges and become unstoppable.

The Formula of Achievement

Chapter 3: **3 Powerful Models that Direct Your Future**

Potential Results[x]   You have clearer and more compelling goals of what you truly want most in 7 important areas of your life.

Chapter 4: **3 Techniques to Change Your State in a Heartbeat**

Potential Results[x]   You summon any states in a blink of an eye and take more control of your life.

Chapter 5:	**5 Steps to Turn Your Dreams into Your Reality**
Potential Results[x]	You maximise your productivity habits that most successful people cannot live without. You then take the fastest route to your dream life.
Chapter 6:	**How to Win and Influence Almost Anyone**
Potential Results[x]	You surround yourself with more successful people and influence them at a higher level to produce even more extraordinary results.

The Psychology of Accelerating

Chapter 7:	**5 Steps to Summon the Best You**
Potential Results[x]	You condition your nervous system to automatically do things that help you achieve your goal faster and easier than you ever thought possible.
Chapter 8:	**Seeing What You Want and Getting What You See**
Potential Results[x]	You tap into your subconscious mind and use creative imagination to come up with ideas that empower you to accelerate the achievement of your dream life.

Chapter 9: **The Psychology of Living Your Dreams Now**
Potential Results[x] — You become who you are destined to be and prepare yourself for greater results. Why wait when you can live your dream life now?

Chapter 10: **How to Effortlessly Attract What Your Heart Desires**
Potential Results[x] — You say goodbye to chasing after what you want when you attract more of what you want in life.

The Art of Fulfillment

Chapter 11: **2 Models for the Happiest You**
Potential Results[x] — You enhance your model of the world so that you feel more fulfilled and achieve greater success.

Results Disclaimer[x]

The above results are based on the experience of my clients. The results of using *Unstoppable You*™ can vary depending on your beliefs, values, circumstances, time commitments, and overall application of *Unstoppable You*™. Based on these factors, it is possible that the use of *Unstoppable You*™ will skyrocket your success or generate no results for you.

The use of *Unstoppable You*™ does not guarantee the improvement of your life. You will not have a more toned body by reading a fitness book without doing more exercise and having a better diet.

No warranty is made with respect to the accuracy or completeness of the information or referenced contained herein, and both the author and the publisher specifically disclaim any responsibility for any liability, loss or risk, personal or otherwise, which is incurred as a consequence, directly or indirectly, of the use and application of any of the contents of *Unstoppable You*™. Anything that you apply from *Unstoppable You*™ is done at your own risk. You are 100% responsible for your failure and success.

Foreword

I am Peter Sage. I personally spent the last quarter-century immersed in the personal development industry as the top expert in personal development. I have spoken at TEDx and delivered keynotes on 5 continents alongside former President Bill Clinton, Tony Robbins, Sir Richard Branson and many other great achievers.

I have noticed that self-improvement books fall into predominantly two categories. The first and most common are the information based 'how to' type of books which act as a literary tour guide and (hopefully) lead to personal transformation. The information is useful and shows the author was well researched.

However, there also exists a much rarer kind of book. These are the books written by the people who experienced the journey themselves in such a way that their passion for what happened left them with no choice but to shout it from the rooftops and share it with the world. Not for money, fame or the significance or being an author, but from a deeper calling of encouragement and excited contribution, as if their Soul's joy is found in helping others make the journey themselves.

Pitima and I both made the decision to take control of our lives at an early age. We learnt the science of achievement from people who were living the kind of life we wanted to live. We applied what we learnt and skyrocketed our success.

Pitima is living proof of the principles in this book. Her life has been a personal laboratory of study and research on the topic of success. She used herself as a guinea pig, testing thousands of different ideas.

Through her failings and triumphs, she found the success principles. What she shares in this book is based on what has worked in her life, and the lives of many great achievers, including me. She used surprisingly simple strategies to rise from poverty to an incredible level of success.

The way people live their lives can either serve as a warning or an example to us. Pitima is the example! Pitima's journey from the penniless streets of Bangkok to mixing with the upper echelons of society offers a story of hope for millions looking to improve the quality of their lives. Her determination and inspiration left a huge light for the rest of us to follow along the pathway to our own greatness.

You have a dream and a great potential to achieve that dream. You are more capable than you think you are. Your current capacity is just a tip of an iceberg. *Unstoppable You™* is the important manual that teaches you how to unleash your full potential and master your personal achievement with fulfillment. Once you do, there is nothing you cannot obtain or achieve.

Unstoppable You™ lays out a series of steps, thought processes, insights and action points in a compelling, profound and systematic way. You can immediately implement them in your life to produce measurable and sustainable results.

Every little decision and action has shaped your life. A two-millimeter miscalculation can send you wildly off your life's course, a mere two-millimeter readjustment can also bring you right back home. The trick is finding the guide that shows you where your destination is. How you get there faster and easier in a more enjoyable way. How you happily stay on the path with phenomenal progress.

You will be blown away by your incredible achievements when you apply the practical, relatable and effective steps in this book. Whatever challenges you are facing, you can overcome them. Whatever dreams you have, you can accomplish them. *Unstoppable You™* is an essential manual to master your life. You will soon join the ranks of the world greatest giants of success.

May this book be Pitima's greatest legacy that forever lightens the world and hugely benefits mankind!

With Passion, Purpose and Panache!

Peter Sage
Founder of the Million Dollar Secret Series
www.PeterSage.com

Foreword

Are you ready for a major breakthrough to the abundance of wealth, success and happiness?

I am Raymond Aaron. I am the New York Times bestselling author of Chicken Soup for the Parent's Soul™. Over 30 years I focused solely on helping people in all walks of life to create more success. I have shared a stage with former President Bill Clinton, Sir Richard Branson, Donald Trump, Steve Wozniak and many other world class speakers.

I spend time learning with my friends from The Secret movie. I have read many books on personal development, and one of the really good one is **Unstoppable You™**. It is a must-read for all pursuers of success and happiness. It can dramatically and quickly improve the quality of your life in all areas, with lasting results.

I have a confession to make. I am not only Pitima's close friend, but I am also one of Pitima's biggest raving fans. I have studied her extraordinary work. I truly believe that spending even 5 minutes with Pitima will be an unforgettable life-changing experience that you cannot afford to miss. I love spending time with her and learning from her.

Pitima is best in class in the realm of human behaviour, personal development and peak performance. She can remarkably unleash your full potential, show hidden resources and guide you to achieve your biggest dreams.

Pitima's fascinating story, from being penniless to being a top high achiever, moves my soul, touches my heart and inspires me to take more action. She refused to settle for anything less than she is capable of being, doing, having and giving. Pitima gives hope to all of us to fulfil our destiny in our own way, by being a great example of someone who defied the odds, ignored naysayers and ended up living her dreams.

The success principles in this book are used by self-made millionaires, great innovators, top entrepreneurs and high achievers including me. When you apply them, you can overcome any challenges and live your dream life.

You will be able to create clear compelling visions, master your emotions, produce action plans and connect with millionaires. You will have tools and techniques that accelerate the achievement of your dreams, such as affirmation, visualisation, acting "as if" and law of attraction. You will live your biggest dreams with the ultimate fulfillment in the level that you could never dream of.

Unstoppable You™ is that detailed guide to creating the life that you desire and deserve. Read this book in its entirety, apply what you learn and experience your life transforming into a masterpiece filled with an abundance of success and happiness. I know you will experience the best life has to offer.

Raymond Aaron
New York Times Bestselling Author of Chicken Soup for the Parent's Soul™

In Gratitude

To **my mother,** thank you for being the greatest mother and role model. I have learnt so much from you. Thank you for all challenges that trained me to become better since I was a kid. You are the number one contributor behind my success. You bring out the very best in me. I treasure your tremendous love and support. I can never thank you enough for everything you have done for me. I deeply appreciate you.

To **Tony Robbins,** thank you for your wisdom that influences my thoughts and shapes my life in a more powerful and empowering way. The quality of my life has been improved and my dreams have come true because of you. Every time we meet, you create an extraordinary experience for me. I am overwhelmed with gratitude. You are a major contributor behind my success and happiness. You inspire me to do the same for others. This book is to my way to pay it forward to make the world a better place.

To the following **mentors and teachers**, thank you so much for shaping my mindset and giving me my greatest strategies to realise my dreams. Thank you Sir Richard Branson, Brendon Burchard, Brian Tracy, Jack Canfield, Harv Eker, Darren Hardy and Les Brown. I salute you all once again.

To my **dear friends** for phenomenal support, Tony Buzan for suggestions on the contents and book cover; Brian Tracy for allowing me to put our picture on the back cover; Richard Tan for the opportunities to learn from the world's greatest teachers who later became my friends because of your help; Greg Johnson for a great friendship and a remarkable support; Chris Hadfield for your kindness, wisdom and support; Alan Bean for an empowering conversation and an inspiration that impossible things happen e.g. walking on the moon! Thank you so much. I appreciate you.

To my **publishing team** who helped me make this book a reality, Raymond Aaron for teaching me how to write a book; Cat Willcock for being an amazing book architect; Lisa Browning for editing; Jesus Cordero for an incredible book cover. I love this book!

To **my clients** who believe in me, thank you for sharing your dreams, struggles and success. The stories you shared with me were incredible. I have learnt much from your heroic efforts in overcoming challenges and your persistence in making your dreams come true.

Thank you for letting me know how much my work has made a difference in your life. You inspired me to write this book to share the principles that I teach and live by. Thank you for your pre-orders even before the book is finished.

To **YOU**, who you are reading this book. Thank you for picking up this book. It is the most honourable privilege to share my ideas, tools and strategies with you. You are the reason I wrote this book. Your desire to achieve greater things will empower you to live an even better life with more fulfillment.

To **YOU**, who picked up this book for your loved one or recommended this book to your family, friends, relatives and colleagues, you are the light of this world. Thank you for making the world a better place by lifting up your loved ones. The world has more success and happiness because of you.

To **YOU**, who wrote encouraging emails or spoke to me in person, you are the oxygen to my work. Your feedback means the world to me. I am humbled to know how I make my work even better, and how I made a positive difference in your lives. Thank you!

My Inspiration for Writing *Unstoppable You*™

"If a man for whatever reason has the opportunity to lead an extraordinary life, he has no right to keep it to himself."
Jacques Cousteau

Unstoppable You™ is the life-transformational book of timeless success strategies used by the world's leading inventors, top entrepreneurs and award-winning celebrities to achieve their extraordinary success throughout history. I have been studying these strategies and applying them to my own life. *Unstoppable You*™ has taken me to the next phenomenal level of success and fulfilment, beyond my wildest imagination.

Arnold Schwarzenegger strongly and publicly proved that I am important and worth listening to. I was the only person who he invited to speak in front of over 1,000 people. Read this amazing story in chapter 8: Miraculous Visualisation.

The Spark of *Unstoppable You*™

Like most of you reading *Unstoppable You*™, my life started out in an average way. My parents were poor and divorced. I had to queue for free food. I was almost homeless. I was raised in poverty in Bangkok. My neighbours were soaked in drugs and violence. Everyone, apart from my mother, had a conviction and consistently told me that I would be an unsuccessful penniless drug-addicted school dropout who would forever live in poverty, and did not deserve a bright future.

I chose my own destiny. I received a scholarship every semester, went to New Zealand as an exchange student and represented my university at a national competition in Thailand and an international seminar in Japan. I received a Bachelor's Degree in Engineering from the number one university in Thailand. I then graduated with a Master's Degree in Technology in London. I worked for the world's leading investment bank, JPMorgan, in the very competitive Elite Graduate Program in Technology for high-calibre people before getting promoted. I was a self-made millionaire in Thai currency before I was 25. Like most of you, the most important person behind my success is my mother who has trained and supported me.

Bill Clinton delivered a great speech prior to my dinner. I socialised with top entrepreneurs (Tony Robbins), Hollywood producers (Peter Berg), Oscar Award winners (Arnold Schwarzenegger), Grammy Award winners (Michael Bolton), world champions (Dominic O'Brien), NASA moonwalkers (Buzz Aldrin) and other great achievers.

I was invited to join the Royal Enclosure in England. I travelled to my dream countries, stayed at the world's best luxury resorts and dined at the 3 Michelin starred restaurants with my friends who are the founders of multi-million pounds companies as well as managing directors at JPMorgan. I coached people at JPMorgan for peak performance. I was living a life beyond my wildest dreams. But I felt so empty. So I searched for answers.

The Inspiration for *Unstoppable You*™

I learnt from Tony Robbins in a live event and noticed the difference he made to me and others. That was when I found my life mission. My passion is to empower you to live your biggest dreams faster and easier than you could ever imagine. Nothing drives me more than to see you succeed in everything you do and live a life full of the deepest sense of fulfillment.

I am obsessed with unleashing human potential, and the science of success. I have been intensely learning from over fifty books, listening to thousands of hours of audio programs, studying many researches, learning from biographies of extraordinary people, interviewing high achievers and attending over £20,000 seminars to discover the universal strategies for living the life of the ultimate dreams with more success and fulfillment. My life has been dramatically changed since I applied these strategies.

People are inspired by my changes. They asked me to coach them. My initial clients are directors at Fortune 100 companies, corporate employees, investment bankers, entrepreneurs and other high-performance individuals, just like you. My clients then quickly expanded throughout Europe and Asia through referrals. Although I spend a lot of time coaching, my clients have to wait for a long time. So I decided that a better way to help them is to write *Unstoppable You*™ so that they get instant advice, and I help more people.

The Purpose of *Unstoppable You*™

I know you! I may not know you personally, but I know about you. No matter how well you are already doing or how challenged you now may be, deep inside of you there lies a deep desire to do something greater with your life. You want to become more, have more and achieve more than what most people settle for in life.

I know this because you picked up *Unstoppable You*™. You see, you and I are alike. We are dreamers and achievers. Your desire to expand has brought you to this book. Some people are afraid of the concepts in this book. They are afraid of having big goals and taking massive actions. So they settle in the comfort of mediocrity. But that is not you.

If you are still reading this, chances are that you do not want to sit behind a desk until you are 60, and retire poor. You want to join the top 3 percent of people who have 97 percent of the wealth. Whether your dream is escaping the rat race, having financial freedom, living your dream lifestyle, being in a more passionate relationship, having a better career, having a more successful business or having better health; the purpose of this book is to empower you to achieve the life of your wildest dream.

Unstoppable You™ shares with you what made a huge positive difference in my life and others. I sincerely hope that you find the tools, strategies, stories and step-by-step guides in this book to be as empowering for you as they have been for me.

I Believe in You

I believe that you can achieve your ultimate dream faster and easier in a more enjoyable way, especially when you apply these strategies. I believe that you have a phenomenal potential which can transform your wildest dreams into your extraordinary reality. I believe that you have within you the unstoppable force. Once it is unleashed, you can overcome any obstacles and achieve anything that your heart desires. It is time to awake the superhero within you. Believe in yourself. I believe in you.

Be Unstoppable and Live Your Dreams.

Pitima Tongme
www.youtube.com/watch?v=m11ZDHLivbk

A WARNING

*"No matter how great the talents or efforts,
some things just take time.
You can't produce a baby in one month by
getting nine women pregnant."*
Warren Buffett

Success is never a given. It has to be earned with hard work, self-discipline, commitment and sacrifice. You have a choice to pay the major price of regrets by not taking actions, or enjoy the enormous rewards of success by taking actions.

I challenge you not only to do whatever it takes to read *Unstoppable You*™ in its entirety (unlike the masses who quit), but also to apply what you learn in simple ways to create more success-driven habits toward your main goal every day.

Success will not happen overnight. It takes time, effort, persistence and patience. At the beginning, you may wonder why your progress is slow, or why there is no result even after you apply these strategies. I encourage you not to give up on your dreams.

These strategies may not suit everyone. Apply what works for you. Taking action is necessary for you to produce the results you desire. I challenge you to make your life a masterpiece. I challenge you to live the life of your ultimate dreams.

PART ONE

THE POWER

OF

FREEDOM

Chapter 1
Victor of Your Destiny
7 Strategies to Escape the Wheel of Your Demons

*"The ultimate measure of a man is not
where he stands in moments of comfort and convenience,
but where he stands at times of challenge and controversy."
Martin Luther King*

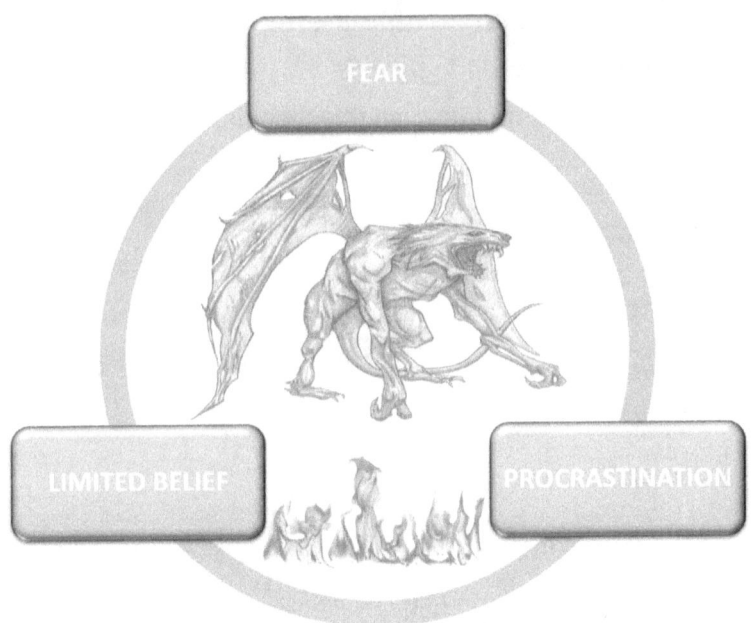

The reason why you are not living your dream life right now is because something stops you internally or externally. When you are a master at handling challenges, what can stop you? The answer is nothing. If nothing can stop you, you become unstoppable. In this chapter, you are going to turn the spotlight upon 3 causes that stop you and 7 cures that conquer them.

Before you overcome what stops you, you must first find the real root cause. When people do not get what they deserve, they often blame other people or circumstances. You have a choice to be the victim of your circumstances or the victor of your destiny. You can fix anything when you accept that the root cause is you. Either you cause the problem or you are not resourceful enough to fix it. If you do not like something, change it. If you cannot change it yet, change your attitude or move on to something else.

The important thing is not to settle until you get what you are worth. The dream is yours when you are willing to take hits and keep moving forward, no matter how hard and how many hits you take. When you are willing to pay any price, you forever live the life of your dreams.

The 3 common demons that prevent people from living the life that they desire and deserve are:
- Fear
- Procrastination
- Limited Belief

Demon#1: Fear

*"When I look back on all these worries, I remember
the story of the old man who said on his deathbed that
he had had a lot of trouble in his life,
most of which had never happened."*
Winston Churchill

Fear is Fantasized Experiences Appearing Real. It is nothing but an imagination. You have a choice to Forget Everything And Run, or Face Everything And Rise.

What Do You Fear?

Fear of Not Being Enough
- Fear of failure
- Fear of imperfection
- Fear of the change: stop or start

Fear of Not Being Loved
- Fear of rejection
- Fear of being alone
- Fear of being different

Is it some of the above? All of the above? Maybe you can add a few more to the list. It is okay. You are not the only one who feels afraid. Join the crowd! People who live their dream life also have fear, but they do not let the fear stop them. The same can be true for you.

"Our deepest fear is not that we are inadequate. Our deepest fear is that we are powerful beyond measure. It is our light, not our darkness that most frightens us. We ask ourselves, Who am I to be brilliant, gorgeous, talented, fabulous? Actually, who are you not to be? Your playing small does not serve the world. There is nothing enlightened about shrinking so that other people will not feel insecure around you.

We are all meant to shine, as children do. We were born to make manifest the glory of God that is within us. It is not just in some of us; it is in everyone. And as we let our own light shine, we unconsciously give other people permission to do the same. As we are liberated from our own fear, our presence automatically liberates others."

Marianne Williamson

Why Do We Fear?

*"When you hold onto your history, you
do it at the expense of your destiny."*
Bishop TD Jakes

Since we were children, with love, our parents told us to be careful and not take risks. When we make a mistake, people make fun of us. We do not want to look foolish in front of others. We want to be loved and accepted. When we do not do well, we receive a punishment. No one wants a punishment.

> "The only thing we have to fear is fear itself."
> Franklin Roosevelt

Some of us failed in the past, and continue to live there. They do not try again because they want to avoid the feeling of disappointment. This programs us to live in fear and not take risks. But the biggest risk is not taking any risks. The key is to embrace the risk, face your fear and go for what you want. The best way to move forward is to let go of your past result which does not empower you.

What Fear Can Do to You

> "Fear defeats more people than
> any other one thing in the world."
> Ralph Waldo Emerson

Fear kills your imagination and blinds you from seeing the truth that there is nothing forever standing between you and your desire. Fear reduces your ability, changes your behaviour and paralyses your decision-making. Fear stops you from taking action, prevents you from getting what you want, and leads you to unhappiness. If you focus on fear, you will make up a story to make you feel fear even though there is nothing to fear. The hell on earth is living in fear.

Fear of Not Being Enough

"No man ever became great or good except
through many and great mistakes."
William Gladstone

It is okay to fail. Failure is the beginning of success. If you have not failed, your goal is not big enough. Sometimes failure leads to a loss. Many people fear losing, particularly money or relationship. But things are never lost. They transform. A loss is transformed into a gain in lesson. A failure is a success in finding what does not work. It is a step closer to success.

"Failure is simply the opportunity to begin again,
this time more intelligently."
Henry Ford

When the result is not what you expected, you learn from it and improve upon it until you get the result that you want. When you learn from your setback and do not make the same mistake, you become wiser and ready to succeed even more.

"Don't compare yourself with anyone.
If you do so, you are insulting yourself."
Bill Gates

You live in a shadow of someone else when you feel that you are not good enough. When you compare yourself to someone, who you think is better than you, you are blind to seeing that what is great in them is also inside of you. If you do not appreciate yourself, no one will. If you are not grateful for your gift, it will soon disappear. Show the world how great you are. You are not here to live in a shadow. You are here to shine while standing on the shoulder of giants.

Imagine you are a junior employee of a Fortune 500 company and you have to give a talk to a group of kindergarten students on a topic on which you are an expert. Can you do it? Of course, you can. Now let us replace the students with the CEO of the Fortune 100 companies. Are you feeling a little nervous this time? If so, why? Is it because you just raised their worth while decreasing yours?

No one is worth being put on a pedestal. All you have to do is realise that what is great in them is also inside of you, be your best self and make continuous improvement. Progress is better than perfection. This wisdom is also a cure for jealousy.

Fear of Not Being Loved

Enjoy your own company. Do not chase or change so that people will like you. You waste your time and energy when you focus on people who want to leave you. Use your time to invest in people who love the real you. When you are your best self and do your own things extremely well, the right people will come and stay.

When you raise the level of self-love high enough, you do not need anyone to love you in order for you to feel love. Imagine that you had your last £10 on a table and someone just stole it. You would have a negative feeling, would you not?

Imagine again that you just won a lottery and you had £1,000,000 on the same table. The same person stole £10 from £1,000,000. How would you feel this time? If I were you, I would give him more money if he were desperate for £10. Love is the same. When you love yourself more, you give more love to others and feel love even if someone takes love away from you.

3 Strategies for Moving Beyond Fear

"The pain is not due to the thing itself, but to your estimate of it; and this you have the power to revoke at any moment."
Marcus Aurelius

It is normal to fear; we all do, but do not let fear stop you. Fear is nothing more than a state of mind. You have a choice to focus on faith instead of fear. You will learn how to master your state in chapter 4: Instant State Transformation. Fear will not go away. But you can embrace it and do whatever you have to do.

There are 3 strategies to help you move beyond fear:
- The Wiser of the Wisest
- The Unshakable Confidence
- The Warrior in Your Larger Life Zone

1. The Wiser of the Wisest

"Risk comes from not knowing what you are doing."
Warren Buffett

When you enter unfamiliar territory, it is okay to feel fear. But if you know that you can handle whatever happens, what will you fear? The answer is nothing. You move beyond fear by having more education. Learning does not start or stop at school. Continuous learning is important.

Fear creates the illusion that things appear bigger than they actually are. If you label something as fear, it creates fear when there is nothing to be afraid of. Many people mistake a fear with a concern. It is much easier to break down a concern than it is a fear. Concern can be cleared when you have enough knowledge. Fear can be overcome when you replace a feeling of fear with a problem-solving attitude.

> *"I do not think much of a man
> who is not wiser today than he was yesterday."*
> *Abraham Lincoln*

A way to overcome fear is to grow yourself so that you are bigger than any problems. Do not pray to have no problems. No challenge lasts forever for someone who does not give up and who refuses to be stopped by anything. Problems are gifts when you prepare yourself to be bigger than any challenges. You break through challenges and become a better person with a greater capability.

> *"The significant problems we face cannot be solved by
> the same level of thinking that created them."*
> *Albert Einstein*

The size of a challenge is never an issue. What matters is the size of you. On a scale of 1 to 10, 1 being the lowest, imagine that the problem is at level 3 and your ability is at level 1. The problem seems like a big problem.

Now imagine that you grow into a level 5 capacity and look at the same level 3 challenge. Magically, the identical challenge is now small. Finally, imagine that you work hard on yourself and become a level 10 person. The same level 3 puzzle may not even be registered in your brain as a problem.

*"If a man empties his purse into his head,
no man can take it away from him.
An investment in knowledge always pays the best interest."*
Benjamin Franklin

The way to grow is to educate yourself more. Learn from books and people who succeeded before you. The more you grow and the bigger goals you have, the greater challenges you are going to face. The key to success is to keep growing.

2. The Unshakable Confidence

"With confidence, you have won before you have started."
Marcus Garvey

The unshakable confidence is about developing more trust in yourself, more faith in others and more expectation of luck. If you do not have confidence in your own ability, you will not be successful or happy. If you have an absolute trust in your ability and know that you can overcome any obstacles, what will you fear? The answer, again, is nothing.

You have more capability than you ever dreamed of. You have more potential than you can ever develop in a lifetime. You just have to develop more trust in your ability to handle whatever comes your way. Be your best self, focus on your strengths, create more wins and maintain winning habits.

When you have more faith in other people, you will see more miracles through them. Life is magical when you help someone just because you can. Just as you never give up on yourself, you should not give up on others. When someone makes a mistake, you should give them a second chance, raise them up and be a rainbow in their cloud. When there is cloud in your life, believe that you will meet someone who can help you remove the cloud or raise you above it. The sun is always shining no matter how cloudy it seems.

When you expect more luck, you will experience life at a better level. Believe that miracle, god, universe or whatever you define will make your experience turn out well. The more you learn and the more extra miles you go, the more luck you will find.

3. The Warrior in Your Larger Life

"One of the greatest discoveries a man makes,
one of his great surprises, is to find
he can do what he was afraid he could not do."
Henry Ford

Now you have more education and have more trust in yourself, the next step is to expand your comfort zone. No one dies of discomfort, but living in your comfort zone kills you slowly. You might have heard the story of the boiling frog.

If a frog is placed in boiling water, it will immediately jump out. But if it is placed in a pot, which is filled with room temperature water and slowly heated, it will not perceive the danger. It will stay in the warm water until it is too hot and too late to jump out. It will be cooked to death.

Your dream life is outside your comfort zone. If your goal is to be comfortable, chances are you will never live your dream life. If your goal is live your dream life, you are going to end up living it as well as being comfortable. The quality of your life expands to the extent that you do. Every day, do something that your future self will thank you for even though it is outside of your comfort zone.

Many people do not start because they think that they have to go far beyond their comfort zone at the beginning. If you are afraid to start big, start small and keep expanding. Have you ever questioned why a little thing can make us feel a huge difference?

People can ask for a £5,000 pay raise but £6,000 makes them feel anxious. They can approach their colleagues who are at the same level, but higher levels make them feel nervous. They can speak in front of 10 friends but 10 unknown potential clients make them panicky.

This is because of the level of their expectation and standard. Now is the time to raise your standard, do something outside your comfort zone and become more comfortable with the unknown. The quality of your life is in direct proportion to your ability to handle the unknown.

We Have a Problem - Fred Haise

I am fortunate to speak with Freddo about his NASA mission in Space, Apollo 13. I asked if they were afraid when they were floating out in the space further and further away from earth in a cold and complete shutdown rocket, and did not know how to get back to earth. He said they were fine because about 90% of their training at NASA was to train outside their comfort zone and to deal with failure e.g. when nothing was working. They also trusted people at NASA. There were four teams at NASA for each mission. In addition to that, NASA has experts all over the world who they can quickly contact and ask them to rapidly come up with a solution for any problems. NASA also has a lots of procedures to deal with any kind of failures. He laughed before adding, "But not just this one."

Demon#2. Procrastination

*"Procrastination is like a credit card:
it is a lot of fun until you get the bill."*
Christopher Parker

All of us have a dream but many of us let the dream die inside. We fool ourselves that our dream will come true one day. But that day never arrives because every day we delay our actions by a day. How often and how soon 'not now' becomes 'never'. Before you realise it, your dream is lost forever.

You have a need to avoid pain and a desire to gain pleasure. You do more to avoid pain than you do to gain pleasure. You look forward to an immediate impact rather than a longer-term impact whether pain or pleasure comes first.

You sometimes do not follow through to achieve your goal even though it gives you a tremendous amount of pleasure when you accomplish it. It is because you believe that taking immediate action would be more painful than delaying the action. In short, if pain comes first, you will procrastinate.

There are 3 strategies to help you overcome procrastination:
- The Pain to Power
- The Pain to Pleasure
- The Pleasure to Prosperity

1. The Pain to Power

Have you ever experienced this? You had been putting something off for so long because you did not want to go through the pain of taking action. Then one day the pain of not taking action was more painful than taking action. So you took action even though you had to go through pain.

Have you ever studied overnight to take the next day exam or worked overnight to prepare a presentation for tomorrow? Why did not you study or prepare the presentation a long time ago when you had more time? Did studying or preparing mean going to a bit of pain so you would rather be doing something else which gave you more pleasure?

Why did you study or prepare at the last minute? Was it because you felt that you would experience more pain if you did not study or prepare? So you would rather study or prepare the presentation than getting an F or getting fired.

Pain has a threshold. When you reach the threshold, you will say, "That is it! Enough! No more! I have had it! Never Again! This must change now!" When you hit this threshold and decide that you are not willing to settle for this massive pain anymore, you will take a less painful action to overcome the massive pain. By understanding this, you can bring the unbearable pain forward and add urgency to it to motivate yourself to take action now.

2. The Pain to Pleasure

"Persons with comparatively moderate powers will accomplish much if they apply themselves wholly and indefatigably to one thing at a time."
Samuel Smiles

Another reason why you do not take action is because the task is so big, and overwhelms you. When you take on a big complex task, you do not know where to start. It seems to take a lot of time or it looks painful even before you start.

A way to reduce this pain and to encourage action is to cut down a big task into simpler and smaller tasks. It is easier to do a small piece of a large project than to start on the whole project which overwhelms you.

When you accomplish a small task, it gives you a sense of achievement and satisfaction. When you feel happier and more powerful, you will have more motivation to do another task, and then another task. When you keep this momentum going, you will complete all tasks in a more enjoyable way.

The key is to break a task down, keep it simple, start small and keep the momentum going until the whole project is completed. If the tasks still overwhelm you, you are in a perfectionist state of mind or an idealist mode. The required tasks are usually not as many as you think. Put your tasks into 3 categories: must, should or could. Start with "must" to complete the core requirements. Then enhance it later.

3. The Pleasure to Prosperity

Use procrastination as an inspiration to do what you love. The cause of procrastination is that you are trying to do something that you do not love. Chances are you may not get it done, you may not enjoy doing it or you may not get as great a result as you could.

Procrastination alerts you to what you should or should not be doing according to what you love. When you procrastinate, your mind tells you that you should not be doing it because it is not you. There are 7 ways to overcome procrastination, do less of what you do not love and do more of what you love.

7 Ways to Do More of What You Love

- Automate, eliminate or delegate the task to others.
- Swap work with your colleague or house chores with your family in a way that benefits both of you.
- Do a task in a more inspiring way, which produces the same result, by changing the process, location, time or people with whom you interact.

- Alter your perception of the task. It is a mind trick. When you do something that you do not love, think of a similar activity that you love. For an example, if you do not love washing dishes but you love dancing, think that you are dancing instead of washing the dishes, similar to the Karate Kid movie. While washing the dishes, why don't you turn your music on, sing along and dance with your whole body – just the way you love it?
- Use your "why" as your inspiration. If the reason why you want it big enough, your "why" will pull your towards your goals. Find out more about this in the Precious Treasure Guardian section in chapter 2: Remarkable Breakthrough.
- Question your original thought if you think you are stuck due to a limited resource. Find out more about this in the Unlimited Resources section in chapter 2: Remarkable Breakthrough.
- Change to do what you love, what you have a passion for and what inspires you at the core level. It is something that keeps you up at night because you love doing it so much. It is something that you cannot wait to get up start doing.

Demon #3. Limited Belief

"The only thing standing between you and your goal is the bullshit story you keep telling yourself as to why you cannot achieve it."
Jordan Belfort

The majority of what stops you comes from limited beliefs which are supported by false references. References come from what you experience, see and hear through other people, events, news, books and movies.

When some people tell you that you cannot reach your goal because you are not good enough, they are the ones who are not good enough for you. Have you ever wondered what makes them an expert on your potential and capability? When you are aware that these non-supportive beliefs are not your perspectives, you can get rid of them easily.

Do not let anyone, in particular yourself, tell you that you cannot achieve what you want. You cannot succeed if you keep creating false stories about why you cannot do it, "I cannot be that. I am not good enough. It will never work. I have tried everything. There is nothing else I can do." Why make excuses when you can make it happen?

The Flip Side of the Wheel

*"Within you right now is the power to
do things you never dreamed possible.
This power becomes available to you just
as soon as you change your beliefs."*
Dr. Maxwell Maltz

Your beliefs do not only determine your outcomes but also turn off or on any opportunities and resources that are available to you. The reality is not a reality, but a perception of the reality. You have a choice to discard the beliefs that hold you back and to create more empowering beliefs that support the achievement of your goals.

A way to do it is to question your old limited beliefs. What has it cost you in the past? What will it cost you in the future? What are your new empowering beliefs? What pleasure are you gaining from the new beliefs? Model powerful beliefs of those who succeeded before you.

Focus on your past results when you succeeded. If you succeed once, it is easier to succeed again. Register a future positive reference in your brain by seeing yourself achieving the result again and again in your mind, feel a tremendous amount of positive emotion and make it real. You will learn more about changing your beliefs in the Hell and Heaven Conditioning in chapter 2: Remarkable Breakthrough.

BONUSES: Master Your Brain™ and Maximise Your Success™

Watch Tony Buzan, Inventor of Mind Mapping, reveal strategies on how you can overcome fear, procrastination and limited belief in a more creative way.

Listen to Greg Johnson, NASA astronaut for 2 Space Missions, explain how astronauts overcome fear and how you can do the same to maximise your success.

www.BeTheUnstoppableYou.com/BookVIP

Chapter 2
Remarkable Breakthrough
3 Strategies to Awaken the Hero within You

*"Whether you think you can, or
you think you can't, you're right."*
Henry Ford

If you do not have what you want, it is because something stops you from achieving it. The story is that you do not have the right resource, mindset or reason. You are waiting for something to happen or for someone to remove these false impediments.

The truth is that you are the one who you have been waiting for. You make your dream become your reality. You have within you the greatest warrior who can conquer any challenges and enable you to live your dream life. In this chapter, you are going to learn how to overcome any obstacles, including the things that others are certain are impossible, by using *Awakening the Hero within You™*.

When you are aware of your unconscious resources, you can go up, down, around or through any obstacles until you get what you want. When you have a right mindset, you can accomplish anything. When you have a right reason, you are unstoppable.

Awakening the Hero within You™

- The Unlimited Resources
- The Hell and Heaven Transformation
- The Precious Treasure Guardian

1. The Unlimited Resources

*"To ask the right question is already
half the solution of a problem."*
Carl Jung

You have resources, more than you ever realise, inside of you or through others, for everything. You may forget them or not yet recognise them. The easiest way to reveal your resources is to make an inventory of all of the resources that you already have. They can be character traits, beliefs, people, money, tools, strategies, skills, knowledge, experience or whatever.

Can you think of the time when you used these resources most skilfully through the achievement of personal goal, finance, relationship, work or hobby? What did you think, feel and do? What was it about that situation that accelerated your achievement? How can you leverage these resources in your current situation?

*"The important thing is not to stop questioning.
Curiosity has its own reason for existing."*
Albert Einstein

Unleash more resources by asking a better question and coming up with a more creative answer. Here are examples:

- How can you substitute, combine, adapt, magnify, minimise, add, remove, reuse, repurpose or rearrange your existing resources to get the new resource that you want? A classic movie to learn from is Apollo13 when they used existing resources to bring the astronauts back to earth safely.
- Who can benefit from you when you reach your goal? They can be your suppliers, business partners or other beneficiaries.
- How can you add more values and create a wider impact before, during or after you reach your goal? You can do it by using your existing resource before you achieve your goal or a new resource after you accomplish it.
- Who has a comprehensive list of your potential suppliers, clients or business partners? How can you directly or indirectly add more value to them and leverage their lists?
- Who do your contacts know? How can you add value to them?

- How can you add value to someone by getting the value from someone else and then give the value to who you can add another value?

As you can see from the above questions, people are the greatest resource. When you deal with people, make sure you follow the guidelines below:

- Only deal with people who have authorisation to do a deal with you. They can be the CEO or the owner.
- Show them that the perceived value is much more than what they are after. You just ensure that what you offer is something that they need or want. It can have an immediate impact or a longer term impact.
- Let them know in advance that this is a one-time offer only. If they say no or take more than a certain time to think, you are going to their competitors and help them increase their competitive advantage. If they say no, you can simply go to another organisation.

You Can Have Anything When You Are Creative Enough - Peter Sage

My friend, Peter Sage, is the co-founder of Space Energy. He excels at asking better questions and developing greater strategies. Matt owned a flower stall. He needed £20,000 to buy another stall. Peter asked Matt questions and suggested that

Matt could offer his supplier a double wholesale from £250,000 to £500,000 a year.

Matt could give his supplier an exclusive right for £5,000 and offer that £5,000 now to the stall seller as a premium. Over a year, Matt could pay the seller £20,000. If Matt could not pay £20,000 within a year, the seller could have his stall back.

The seller could earn £5,000 a year from £20,000. This rate was higher than putting money in a bank. The supplier could sell £250,000 more within a year for £5,000 which was cheaper than an advertisement to gain £250,000 more in sales. Matt could have the new stall without having to borrow the money against his house.

2. The Hell and Heaven Transformation

A way to break through a limited belief is to link an unbearable and urgent pain to your old limited belief and link a massive and immediate pleasure to your new empowering belief. Here are 4 simple steps:

- Use Pain as a Motivation
- Disassociate from Limited Belief
- Use Pleasure as an Inspiration
- Condition Yourself

1) Use Pain as a Motivation

When you associate enough pain to the results of not taking action, you will take action. Start by writing down what you want and the limited beliefs that stop you from getting it. Then associate a massive pain to the limited beliefs. Can you feel that not only has it cost you pain in the past but it is also costing you an unbearable pain now, and it only brings you an unimaginable pain in the future?

What are the inconsistencies or conflicts in your belief, behaviour, value, standard and identity? Living against your own values is heart-breaking. Knowing that you fail to live up to your own standards is unbearable. There is nothing more painful than having your identity taken from you.

For example, if you cannot stop smoking or eating fat food, visit a shelter to see the worst thing that happens to people who smoke or eat fat food. When you are there, talk to them to realise negative impacts to their health, body, emotion, finance, relationship and lifestyle as well as additional costs to their family and loved ones.

Alternatively, visit an intensive wing of a hospital to observe patients confined to oxygen tents and imagine that it could be you if you continue doing what you are now. Are you willing to pay the price? If not, link such an intensive pain to your old beliefs to motivate you to get rid of them forever.

If you do not act now, what will happen and how will you feel in the next 1-10 years? What will it cost you emotionally, mentally, physically, socially and financially? What will it cost you, your family and people who you care about? Are you willing to pay the price that it has been charging you? If not, take new action now.

2) Disassociate from Limited Belief

Write down what pleasure you gain by not taking action and find a new way to gain the same pleasure without having a negative consequence. Then disassociate your old beliefs by interrupting your pattern so as to remove false references.

Have you ever been deeply talking to a friend, had someone interrupt you, then come back wondering, "Where were we?" Of course you have. You can start monitoring your thoughts, habits and actions. If you notice a non-supportive thought or behaviour, interrupt it immediately by doing something different or unexpected.

We sometime have a doubtful thought in our head but we do not have to believe or listen to it. When you hear a little voice that weakens you, replace it with more empowering one or just sing a song. It is not possible to have two voices or two thoughts at the same time.

3) Use Pleasure as an Inspiration

You cannot get rid of something without replacing it with something else. You must associate tremendous pleasure to new action. Write down what pleasure you gain emotionally, mentally, physically, socially and financially by taking action. What other benefits that you, your family and your loved ones can have?

Fast forward to a year, or a decade, imagine and feel the ultimate pleasure when you take action and achieve your dream. Bring the extreme pleasurable feeling to the present moment and feel it right now so that it is so real, intense and immediate in a way that you cannot wait to take action.

Here is an example. If you believe that you cannot succeed because you are a woman, do the following:

1) Do a funny move whilst saying, "I cannot succeed because I am a woman."
2) Clench fists against your chest, swing your arm away from your body and say "Bullshit" out loud.
3) Step forward, feel the enormous amount of an empowering emotion and say the following sentence even louder, "Because I am a woman, I have more resources and opportunities available to me that any man could ever dream of!"

4) Anchor your new belief with an empowering move.
5) Repeat steps 1-4 a few times.

4) Condition Yourself

Consistently repeat these steps again and again with a remarkable emotional intensity. Gift yourself by making this conditional process your new habit. Do not wait until you achieve your final goal. Reward yourself immediately every time you make progress. Your reward can be self-praise, a gift or a treat. If you have gone a day without smoking or if you eat a healthy food instead of a fat food, give yourself a pat on the back and say, "great job!" When you go an extra mile, give yourself an extra reward.

3. The Precious Treasure Guardian

*"You can have anything you want if you want it badly enough.
You can be anything you want to be,
do anything you set out to accomplish if
you hold to that desire with singleness of purpose."
Abraham Lincoln*

It is never a question of your capability. There is a force inside of you. Once unleashed, you can accomplish anything that you desire. The way to unleash the unstoppable force within you is to discover your why. The five iterations of asking why are generally sufficient enough to get to a real why.

Why do not you already have it? Say you want to earn £100,000 a year, but for the last 5 years you were only earning £50,000. You might say that the maximum pay for this type of job is only £50,000. So you are probably in the wrong vehicle. You want to consider other options.

Why would you stay in the same job for 5 years even though the pay was 50% less than what you wanted? Maybe fear or lack of education? How about learning how to deal with challenges and get more education?

Whatever it takes, you have to overcome what stops you. There is a good chance that the "why not" for this is the exact same "why not" for other things. Find out what it is and get rid of it once and for all.

You can increase your chance of getting what you want when you know why you want it so badly in a logical and emotional way. Your reasons are stronger when you have answers for all the following 3 questions:

- What is your burning desire to achieving your goal?
- What is the cost that you have to sacrifice if you do not get your result?
- What is the most desirable reward that you gain when you accomplish your goal?

Hernando Cortez aimed to seize the great treasures in Mexico. Once he landed in Mexico, he unloaded his men and told them to burn the ships that carried them. He said, "if we are going home, we are going home in their ships." It is "die" or "win".

Cortez conquered and succeeded in something where others had failed for six centuries. Why? It is because he and his men had a strong reason to win. When you have a strong enough reason, you can get anything you want.

What is your "why"? If you have not found something worth dying for, you have not found something worth living for. When you have a bigger vision, you will face a bigger challenge. Your "why" will keep you going. If you do not have strong enough reasons, you will not sacrifice what you are for what you can become. Find strong enough reasons why you must succeed, and quitting is not an option.

> *"You can do anything in life you set your mind to, provided it is powered by your heart."*
> Doug Firebaugh

The reason must be personal to you. It is something that creates an incredible amount of emotional intensity. If your why is big enough, you will figure out how and you will persist until you get it. When you want it as badly as you want to breathe, you will find a way to get it. Find the reasons.

Let us imagine that there was a 15 centimetres wide and 5 meters long wooden plank on the floor. You would get £500 if you walked on the plank from one end to the other end. Would you do it? Of course, it is an easy £500. What if that same plank was lifted to be on top of a 5 storey building and you were offered the same £500 to walk from one end to another? Would you do it? You probably would not.

Now let us imagine that, at the other end of the plank, was your beloved one: your child, spouse or parents. The building, which your beloved one was in, was on fire. If you did not walk the plank now, your beloved one would be burnt and die instantly. Would you do it now? Absolutely, I would. £500 or not. This example demonstrates the importance of why.

It is good to re-visit your "why" because things keep changing. You will do different things over a period of time. It is easy to get caught up with the change, go with the flow, forget your "why", and end up heading to an opposite direction. When you re-visit your "why", you have an opportunity to assess if what you are doing still fulfils your "why". If not, change what you are doing.

The Heroin in the House - Pitima Tongme

I received a text from my mother while working in London. It was a picture of my house which was surrounded by 2 meters of flood water overnight. It was the worst flood in Thailand over a decade. I called my mother. She said that she and my grandmother were fine.

They did not want to be rescued because they were afraid that thieves would break into the house when they left. They convinced me for a couple of hours, until my battery ran out, that I should not come because I had to be in the 2 meters flood for 50 kilometres before I reached home. There was no boat and I could not swim.

I visualised the worst thing that could happen: my family would drown. My family is my why. I could not forgive myself if I let that happened and I did nothing about it. I had to rescue my family. It seemed impossible but quitting was not an option.

I approached John, the legendary director who was extremely intelligent and resourceful. He is also my great friend who treats me exceptionally well and always empowers me to succeed even more. He always makes time to be with me when I require his help. I showed him the picture. He asked about my rescue plan. I did not have an approach yet but my goal was to do whatever it took to rescue them.

I booked the first flight to Bangkok and headed to the airport. During my journey to the airport, I received a call from Colin in an emergency team. John called them and they offered a rescue mission. Before my plane landed, my family was rescued and waited for me at JPMorgan office in Bangkok.

My family was covered in bruises and cuts because of leeches and snakes. As soon as they saw me, they shouted, "my heroine", hugged me and cried. I gave them treats and took them to a 2 executive bedroom suite on 40th floor in a great hotel. They absolutely loved it.

**BONUSES: Master Your Brain™ and
Maximise Your Success™**

If you think you are not creative enough, think again. Creativity is seeing things from different perspectives. Your brain is more powerful beyond measure. Watch Tony Buzan, Inventor of Mind Mapping, teach you how to be more creative and unleash more resources to overcome any obstacles.

Listen to Greg Johnson, NASA astronaut for 2 Space Missions, about how you can be more resourceful and increase your chance of being the top 1% in your industry.
www.BeTheUnstoppableYou.com/BookVIP

PART TWO

THE FORMULA

OF

ACHIEVEMENT

40

Chapter 3
Irresistible Life Design
3 Powerful Models that Direct Your Future

"Where there is no vision, the people perish."
Proverbs 29:18

What do you really and ideally want in your life? Better feeling? Better shape? Deeper relationship? Better career? More successful business? More money? More energy? More time? More freedom? Welcome to the Irresistible Life Design chapter. You are going to be the great architect for your life.

Society may predict, but only you determine what your life will be. Before you live the life of your dream, you have to know what your dream life is. If you fail to design your life, you unintentionally design to fail. It is important that you have a vision for your future.

Let us fast forward a year or even a decade. What do you see? Who are you? Where are you? What are you doing? Who are you with? How is your relationship? How is your career or business? How are your finances? What lifestyle do you have? What kind of contribution do you make?

I congratulate you if you can answer all of the above questions. By the end of this chapter, your vision will be enlarged or even changed to a better one. If you cannot answer some of the questions now, you are reading the right chapter. This chapter provides 3 powerful models to help you take better control of your life.

The Pyramid of Life™ - it helps you to shape your future by providing targeted questions so that you discover the possible life vision in different areas of your life.

The SMARTER Goal™ - it helps you to develop a bigger and more compelling vision which unleashes your true mind-blowing potential and magnificently pulls you towards the life of your biggest dreams.

Success Map™ - it provides your brain with very powerful strategies that empower you to make your ultimate dreams become reality faster and easier than you thought possible.

All you have to do in this chapter is dream. Have your wildest and craziest dreams, just like when you were a little kid. Let your imagination run to the place where you have a strong conviction that everything is possible.

The Little Difference that Makes a Huge Difference

> *"Too many people overvalue what*
> *they are not and undervalue what they are."*
> *Malcolm Forbes*

Many people work from 9 AM to 5 PM, come home, cook, watch TV and sleep. They do this every single day, 5 days a week, every week. They sometimes escape their routine by hanging out with friends after work or going somewhere for a short holiday. They look at the price before they order food or buy something. Other people live a little bit differently but the principle is the same. They limit themselves by the price instead of going for what they really want.

They think their life is okay even though they spend most of their time doing what they do not really love or have a real passion for. They unconsciously fool themselves that they love what they do when they actually do not. They feel exhausted and look forward to the end of the day or to the weekend so that they do not have to work.

They want more in life. They know they deserve more. What limits them is their goal, which is to pay their bills, to survive, to make it through the day or to have a good holiday a few times a year. They work in a field they are comfortable with but may not have an absolute passion for, in order to pay for things which they may not even like, to impress people who may not even matter, or to continue living the life doing things they do not want to do. They are trapped making a normal living rather than designing the life that they absolutely love. They lead their next generations to go into the same trap.

High achievers, who dream big, are excited and have a passion for the life they design. They wake up very early and go to bed very late. They look forward to work because they love what they do. They see work as their playground. They can choose not to work but they work 7 days a week with the people they love in the locations of their dreams.

They have everything they have ever wanted in terms of health, relationship, business, finance, lifestyle and more. Their lives are phenomenal. They inspire others to live a similar lifestyle or live the lives of their dreams.

So what is the difference between the former and latter ones? The answer is their vision. Your vision must be big and compelling enough so that you grow to be someone worth becoming in the process of achieving it. If a big vision is important, why do people have a medium size goal for their future, or have no goal at all? They may not know how to set goals properly. They may not notice their progress. They may have been unconsciously conditioned to dream small to protect themselves from danger and disappointment.

They may have dreamed bigger in the past but those dreams have never come true. They may be busy living instead of designing their ideal life. They may fear that, if they achieve bigger things, people will take advantage of them or they will no longer fit in society. Do not let them be you. You are worth more than that. Your life matters.

Your Wildest and Craziest Dreams

"It is a funny thing about life; if you refuse to accept anything but the best, you very often get it."
W. Somerset Maugham

The best way to predict your future is to design it. Now just imagine that today is Christmas Day. As you are walking towards a magic Christmas tree decorated with spectacular lights in your ideal location, you see a big box right in front of you. It is calling and asking you to open it. You are excited about what is inside. You immediately tear the wrapping paper and see an alluring shining yellow lamp. Soon you realise that it is the Aladdin lamp. You rub it and the Genie comes out.

The Genie says, "You can make an unlimited number of wishes. It does not matter how impossible your wishes may seem. I am going to make them come true. Now, make the wildest and craziest wishes."

What are you waiting for? Write down all the things you have ever dreamed of being, doing, having and contributing. Your dreams can be about your health and fitness, personal development, relationship, career, business, finance, life style, home, car, or anything that you really want.

If you consider to live fully with no regrets, what has to happen? If you were about to die today, what images would be worthy to flash before your eyes in your last moment? If you know you are guaranteed to succeed in everything, what do you want? Write them down. Write them down now! If you are going to dream anyway, why not dream big? Do not let your pen stop for 5-15 minutes. Do this exercise now. Write down all the things you want in life.

Your Worthy Goals

"Life will pay whatever price you ask of it."
Tony Robbins

_____

_____

_____

_____

Irresistible Life Design

"I never did a day's work in my life. It was all fun."
Thomas Edison

Before you go on a holiday, you decide what you would like to do, see, experience or even eat. When was the last time you planned your life? You work hard and reward yourself by going on a nice vacation which is a temporary escape from your normal day-to-day life. Why don't you design a life you do not have to escape from?

Before you build a business plan, you should first build your life plan. It is good to first figure out what kind of life you want to have, where you want to live, what you want to do, when you want to work, what type of people you want to be surrounded by, whether you want to travel (and how much and where), what type of environment you want to go to each day, etc. Then fit your business plan around your life plan.

Most people do the opposite. They build the business plan first then figure out how to fit their life and their family around the business plan. They pay too high a price and sacrifice what is really important for too little in return.

Do not waste your time chasing a good life when you can live it. Begin by designing your life and scheduling everything to suit your lifestyle. My friends teach entrepreneurs how to create even more wealth. They schedule each event in a location where they want to go and when they want to go.

They changed the 3 days event from Friday - Sunday to Sunday - Tuesday because they want to watch their sons playing basketball on Saturday. How can you do the same? Now is the time to design your life the way you want it. You have your goals from the previous exercise. It is time to align the goals with the following categories in the Pyramid of Life™.

The Pyramid of Life ™

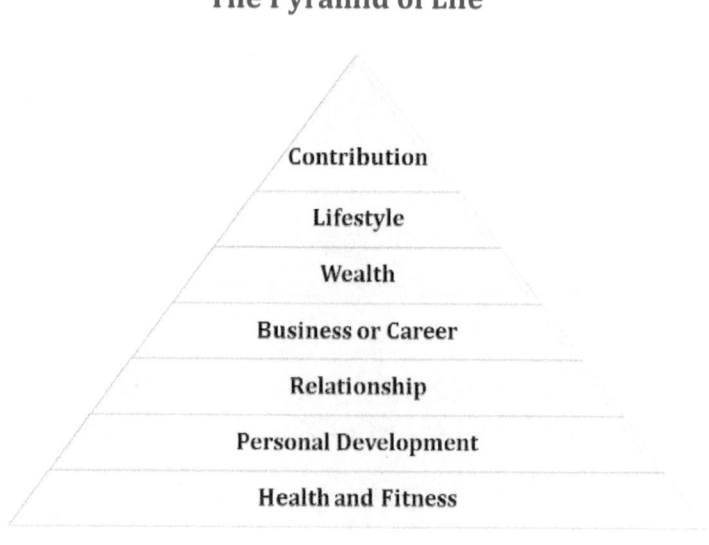

*"All your dreams can come true,
if you have the courage to pursue them."*
Walt Disney

The Pyramid of Life™ represents seven areas that you should consider when you design your future.

It is important to have excellent health, great fitness and an exceptional confidence in your stunning body because your body is the vehicle that you use to carry out your goals. It is the only place you live and you always take it with you.

You must master yourself before you master life. You must better yourself if you want to achieve a better thing. When you have better control of yourself emotionally and physically, your relationship will become much better and more harmonious.

You must have a great business or an outstanding career that generates the level of wealth that you need to fulfil the dream lifestyle. You can have the lifestyle that you want when you have enough wealth to allow you to do so. When you live the life that you want, it is good to give back to society.

The lowest level employee plans her day. A higher level employee plans his month. A manager plans her year. An executive plans a few years ahead. The CEO even plans a decade. You are the architect who plans to build your future; at what level would you plan?

The Pyramid of Life™

"Destiny is not a matter of chance, but of choice."
William Bryan

1. Health and Fitness

Now step into your future, 1-10 years from now:

How satisfied are you with your health, body and fitness?
What are you eating to be healthier?
How are you exercising in a gym or outdoors? How often?
What level of energy are you having?
How are you treating your body?

Step 1:- Write down everything you would like to improve that relates to your health and fitness. It can be something outside the above questions. Your goals can be from your previous exercise or you can create new ones.

_____

_____

_____

Step 2:- Put a timeline against each goal e.g. 1 year, 3 years, 5 years or 10 years. At this stage, you do not need to know how you are going to accomplish them. Just write down the number that you are committed to make it real. A goal is a dream with a deadline. When you set a deadline, your dream will more likely become your reality.

If all your goals are short term, take a longer view of the potential and possibility that your future can hold. If all your goals are longer term, break them down into smaller goals that can make your long term goals come true. A journey of a thousand miles begins with a single step. It is important to have both the first and final steps.

Step 3:- Choose your single and most important one year goal in this category. Choose the goal that, when you accomplish it this year, will bring you the most joy, happiness and fulfillment into your life. You will feel like this year is well invested. If the goal that you most want to accomplish is more than a year goal, think of a smaller goal that, when you accomplish it, will move you closer to your ultimate dream.

My Ultimate Goal for Health and Fitness this Year is:-

_____

2. Personal Development

Now step into your future, 1-10 years from now:

Who are you?
How great are you feeling about yourself?
How well are you managing your emotions?
How efficiently have you managed your time?
What character traits have you enhanced?
What additional knowledge have you gained?
What new skills have you mastered at a higher level?
How has your outlook on life changed to help you become better?
What habits have you fostered that have moved you closer to your dreams?

Step 1:- Like the previous category, write down everything you would like to improve that relates to your personal growth.

_____
_____
_____

Step 2 & 3:- Like the previous category, put a yearly timeline against each item in the above list. Then choose your single and most important one year goal in this category.

My Ultimate Goal for Personal Development this Year is:-

_____

3. Relationship

Now step into your future, 1-10 years from now:

How incredible is your relationship?
What character traits does your partner have?
What is your partner like mentally, emotionally and physically?
How are you fulfilling each other's needs?
How are you treating your soul mate?
How is your sweetheart treating you?

Step 1:- Like the previous category, write down everything you would like to improve that relates to your relationship.

_____

_____

_____

Step 2 & 3:- Like the previous category, put a yearly timeline against each item in the above list. Then choose your single and most important one year goal in this category.

My Ultimate Goal for Relationship this Year is:-

_____

4. Business / Career

Now step into your future, 1-10 years from now:

At which level are you enjoying your career?
What is your ideal career?
Who are you working for?
What position are you holding?
How are you contributing at a higher level?
What kind of positive impact are you having?

How successful do you think you are?
What is your ideal business?

What industry is your business leading?
What goals and missions are you having?
Who are the best clients and JV partners that you are serving?
What amazing result are you creating for them?
Who are you hiring and outsourcing to?

Step 1:- Like the previous category, write down everything you would like to improve that relates to your business or career.

_____
_____
_____

Step 2 & 3:- Like the previous category, put a yearly timeline against each item in the above list. Then choose your single and most important one year goal in this category.

My Ultimate Goal for Business or Career this Year is:-

_____

5. Wealth

Now step into your future, 1-10 years from now:

At what level are you satisfied with your finances?

What has to happen for you to feel wealthy and free?
What is your worth and how do you manage your money?
How much are you having so that you can retire and still have an extraordinary life?
When you have your ideal amount of money, what are you doing with the money?
How much are you investing and generating from each passive income stream?
How much are you putting aside for your ideal lifestyle, your kids' education and your parents' healthcare?

Step 1:- Like the previous category, write down everything you would like to improve that relates to your wealth.

_____
_____
_____

Step 2 & 3:- Like the previous category, put a yearly timeline against each item in the above list. Then choose your single and most important one year goal in this category.

My Ultimate Goal for Wealth this Year is:-

_____

6. Lifestyle

Now step into your future, 1-10 years from now:-

At which level are you satisfied with your lifestyle?
How are you spending your ideal day?
What dream home are you living in e.g. a beachfront house?
What car are you driving e.g. BMW, Porsche or Ferrari?
Where are you travelling to e.g. Bangkok or London?
Are you travelling in business or first class?
What hotels are you staying in?
In what restaurants are you dining?

Who are your friends and business partners?
What types of people are you surrounding yourself with?
Who is helping you to achieve your goals to the next level?
Who are you helping to attain their goals at a higher level?

<u>Step 1</u>:- Like the previous category, write down everything you would like to improve that relates to your lifestyle.

_____
_____
_____

<u>Step 2 & 3</u>:- Like the previous category, put a yearly timeline against each item in the above list. Then choose your single and most important one year goal in this category.

My Ultimate Goal for Lifestyle this Year is:-

_____

7. Contribution

Now step into your future, 1-10 years from now:-

At which level are you satisfied with your contribution?
How are you contributing to your family and relatives?
What is your legacy that makes a difference in people's lives?
How are you continuously contributing?
- Create a charity?
- Donate to charity?
- Volunteer at a charity?

<u>Step 1</u>:- Like the previous category, write down everything you would like to improve that relates to your contribution.

_____
_____
_____

<u>Step 2 & 3</u>:- Like the previous category, put a yearly timeline against each item in the above list. Then choose your single and most important one year goal in this category.

My Ultimate Goal for Contribution this Year is:-

_____

The SMARTER Goal™

You should now have 7 compelling one year goals that absolutely excite and inspire you at the core level. It is time to refine them by using the SMARTER Goal™.

Specific - Your goal must be specific and contain success criteria that you can measure. It must be positive and stated in the present tense. If your goal is "I want to be richer," "richer" is not specific. Both £1 and £1,000,000 make you richer but they are much different.

For an example, change it to "I enjoy increasing the average daily net sale by 20% (£20,000 a day) through an online sales via www.mycompany.com by 25th February 2015 because I need enough capital to invest in another exciting business, www.mycompany2.com."

Motivation - Your goal must be big and compelling enough to motivate and inspire you. Something that keeps you up at night and wakes you up in early morning. Something that you cannot wait to accomplish. Your goal should excite you and pull you toward it like the gravity and the earth.

There are two types of motivation: push and pull. Push requires will power and it never last. What will last is pull. Create a goal that pulls you towards it. It is not something that you lose. It is something that you gain and brings you tremendous pleasure.

If your goal is "I want to lose weight," "losing weight" is not inspiring and it focuses in the wrong area - weight. It tells you what you are going to lose, not what you are going to gain. It is hard to move forward with that.

Instead of the above goal, change to "I enjoy transforming into a head-turning fitness model body (35-25-36" on 14th February 2016) by running in Hyde Park for an hour 3 times a week."

Ambitious - The purpose of setting a goal is not to achieve it but to aim at it. Your goal should be worthy of who you are becoming while achieving it. When you achieve it, it is great. If you have not yet achieved it, you grow to be the best you.

It is not always about achieving your goal. Your journey is more important than your destiny. You feel alive and excited when you make the progress and become a better person.

> *"For what is the best choice, for each individual,*
> *is the highest it is possible for him to achieve."*
> Aristotle

To become great, you must have a great dream, raise your standards, unleash your full potential, utilise all resources, expand your comfort zone, enlarge your identity, do whatever it takes and believe deep down in your heart that you can achieve anything no matter how impossible it seems. Do not confuse "challenge" with "impossible". Challenge means you should work harder or use a different strategy. Everything is possible if you are willing to pay the price for it.

If you know how to achieve your goal, it is too small for you. Raise your expectation and refine your goal. The best goal encourages you to break out of your comfort zone and become comfortable with the unknown. Your ultimate life begins outside your comfort zone. Do not settle for good when you know you deserve the best. Do not set a goal against what you can get done. Set a goal against your life destiny or greater potential.

> *"The greatest danger for most of us is not that*
> *our aim is too high and we miss it,*
> *but that it is too low and we reach it."*
> Michelangelo

Human race would have nothing if we dreamed small. There would be no America, no man landed on the moon, no light bulb, no credit card, no phone, no computer, no internet, no plane, no car, etc. A great achievement begins with a great dream. The human race and your next generation depend on our dreams so, when you dream, you might as well dream big and be outrageous. You have the greatest gifts. Will you use them to make your life the most glorious example for you and your next generation?

Would Tiger Wood be the world's number one golfer if his goal was just to be the best golfer in his city? If your goal is "I want to be the number one swimmer in my city," stretch your goal to be "I am training to be the number one swimmer in my region by 15th December 2015 because I am eager to compete in the Olympic game in 2020." You will achieve so much more by 15th December 2015 even if you are not the number one in the region yet.

If you must feel that you have achieved a goal, have three levels of goal setting:-

- Minimum achievement e.g. increase the sales by 3%
- Big achievement e.g. increase the sales by 10%
- Ambitious achievement e.g. increase the sales by 20%

Relevant - What do you want if money or time is no object? Your goal is clearer and stronger when you look into your heart and figure out what you truly want. Your goal must be relevant to you; not to your parents, children or managers. It is your life that you are living.

> *"There is only one success –*
> *to be able to spend your life in your own way."*
> Christopher Morley

Live the way you truly want. Do not waste your life living in somebody else's dream when you have an opportunity to live the life you love. Do not be afraid to say no to your loved ones or to someone who you assume has power over you. Your time is not guaranteed, and it is limited. Live fully in every moment and enjoy the gift of life on your own terms.

If your goal is "I want to be a doctor because my parents want it," "parents" is not you. Instead, have "I enjoy creating my legacy through a breakthrough business which gives me tremendous pleasure to see over millions of lives improved by 30th July 2020."

Time - Your goal must have a timeframe. Time is a deadline which puts urgency and drives you towards your goals. When you are committed to your goal, a deadline will force you to use all available resources and do whatever it takes to achieve your goal by that date.

If your goal is "I want to donate to a charity this month," "this month" is not a specific. Instead, say "As part of my monthly contribution, I am going to raise and donate £5,000 to Red Cross on 30th December 2015."

Emotion - Why are some goals accomplished but others are not? Emotion is the bridge between your goal and your action. People suggest that goals are fact only, but you are not a robot. You have emotions. Emotions lead to action. Actions lead to results. When you have to accomplish a task, have you ever felt "I do not fancy doing it?" and end up not doing it?

You will achieve your goal faster when you are excited about it and eager to achieve it. You should attach a positive emotion to your goal. What state do you have to be in so that you can achieve it? How will you feel when you get it? The emotion can be exciting, thrilling, feeling alive, etc.

If your feeling is "I am okay to create another product," "okay" is not an inspiring feeling. Alternatively, have "I am so thrilled to launch a wealth training program on 15th July 2016 to help people achieve their financial freedom faster and easier than they ever imagined."

Reason - What is it for you? Why do you want it? Your why is your ultimate power that pulls you towards your goal even through the toughest challenge. The purpose of doing something is bigger than the object that you pursue. The reason should come from both your head and your heart. If your why is big enough, you will figure out how and you will not stop until you get it.

Your reasons are stronger when you have answers for all the following 3 questions:

- What is your burning desire to achieving your goal?
- What is the cost that you have to sacrifice if you do not get your result?
- What is the most desirable reward that you gain when you accomplish your goal?

If your why is "I want to earn more money for a holiday," "holiday" is not strong enough compared to the following example. Your stronger why can be "I have to have £5,000 more on 15th December 2015 to pay for my son's operation.

That money can save his life so that I can live longer with him whom I love so much." It is more likely that you will raise the money by that time because of the latter reason.

To conclude the SMARTER Goal™ is:
S = Specific
M = Motivation
A = Ambitious
R = Relevant
T = Time
E = Emotion
R = Reason

My SMARTER Goals ™ for this Year are:-

1. Health and Fitness
_____
_____

2. Personal Development
_____
_____

3. Relationship
_____
_____

4. Business or Career

_____

_____

5. Wealth

_____

_____

6. Lifestyle

_____

_____

7. Contribution

_____

_____

Dream Saviour

"You will never reach your destination if you stop and throw stones at every dog that barks."
Winston Churchill

Every possibility once seemed impossible. It is important that you protect your goals no matter what others say and how impossible your goals seem to others. Great people do not only have great dreams but they also protect their dreams. I am grateful that Thomas Edison, Henry Ford, the Wright

Brothers and Bill Gates stuck with their vision despite what people believed, how many times they tried or how long they took to accomplish them.

Thomas Edison dreamed of a lamp that could be operated by electricity. He was told by his teacher that he was too stupid to learn anything. Later, he invented the first light bulb.

Henry Ford dreamed of a horseless carriage. He was poor and did not reach high school. Yet, he invented the first car.

The Wright Brothers dreamed of flying. People said we could not fly. Nonetheless, the Wright Brothers built the first plane.

Bill Gates dreamed of a computer in every home. A chairman of IBM once said, "There is a world market for maybe 5 computers." After Bill Gates invented the personal computer, the majority of households today has at least one computer.

Flying With Pleasure - Sir Richard Branson

*"If you aim higher than you expect,
you could reach higher than you dreamed of."*
Richard Branson

Richard Branson is a very inspiring entrepreneur. I love his vision and wisdom. He wanted to fit seatback videos into all

Virgin planes so that everybody could enjoy high quality entertainment. He worked with manufacturers to develop them. The initial estimated cost was about $10 million which he did not have. No airline had ever launched seatback videos before.

He tried to borrow $10 million but he could not find any banks that would lend him the money. So he asked Boeing, "Would you like to supply us with 12 new 747s with the seatback videos in every plane?" They said, "Yes." From failing to get a $10 million loan, he rescued a $2.5 billion loan. Virgin soon had brand new planes with beautiful seatback videos.

From Homeless to Self-Made Millionaire before the Age of 25 - Pitima Tongme

All dreams come true when you are serious about them. I was born in poverty in Bangkok. My family was poor. I queued to eat free food. I was almost homeless many nights. I went to different places at night to find a safe place to sleep.

My neighbours were soaked in drugs and violence. Everyone, except my mother, had a strong conviction and told me that I would be a penniless drug addicted school dropout. But I had a mind-blowing dream.

I graduated with a Bachelor's Degree in Engineering from the top university in Thailand. I then received a Master's Degree in Technology in London. I worked for the world leading investment bank, JPMorgan, in the very competitive Elite Graduate Program in Technology for high-calibre people before getting promoted. I was a self-made millionaire in Thai currency before I was 25.

I was invited to join the Royal Enclosure in England. I socialised with top entrepreneurs (Tony Robbins), Hollywood producers (Peter Berg), Oscar Award winners (Arnold Schwarzenegger), Grammy Award winners (Michael Bolton), world champions (Dominic O'Brien), NASA moonwalkers (Buzz Aldrin) and other great achievers.

I travelled to my dream countries, stayed at the world's best luxury resorts and dined at the 3 Michelin starred restaurants with my multi-millionaire friends. I contribute to people who live on a street and kid's shelters. I am extremely happy and enjoy life at its fullest. A great reality starts with a great dream. Find more details about me on my youtube page, www.youtube.com/user/PitimaTongme.

BONUS: Success Map™

Your goals from this chapter are the first component of Success Map™. To complete the life changing map you must continue to chapter 4, 5 and 6. It is your treat to have instant access to Success Map™ at
www.BeTheUnstoppableYou.com/BookVIP

Chapter 4
Instant State Transformation
3 Techniques to Change Your State in a Heartbeat

*"Fighter pilots know that fear and other concerns
cloud your mind from what is going on and
what you should be involved in."*
Buzz Aldrin

The quality of your life is in direct proportion to the quality of your state. State is your way of being physiologically and emotionally at any moment. Your state determines the perception of your reality. Your perception determines your decision. Your decision determines your action. Your action determines your results.

People do not have the results that they want because they are in a wrong state. They have an illusion that their circumstances control their state. When they lose the control of their state, they lose the results that they want.

*"It is not what happens to you that matters.
It is how you respond to what happens
to you that makes a difference."*
Zig Ziglar

It is time to take back the control of your state, instead of reacting to the environment. You are going to discover how to quickly summon any state to get the results that you want. The secret to success is to master your state. If you do not, everything controls you. If you do, you are in control of your life.

You can change your state by changing your focus, physiology, or communication.

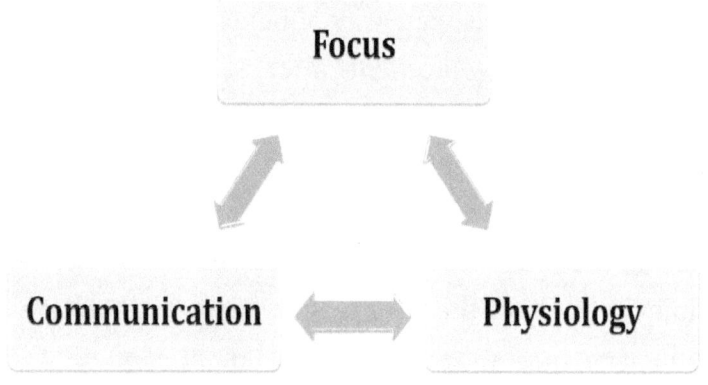

1. The Focus Mastery

"I admit thoughts influence the body."
Albert Einstein

Change your state by changing your focus. You feel bad when you deeply focus on the most horrible thing that happened to you. You feel great when you intensely focus on the most exciting moment that you have had.

Astronauts control their state by choosing what to focus on. My friend, Greg Johnson, was the NASA astronaut who piloted a space shuttle into space twice. During the launch, he saw the phenomenal light, heard the incredible sound, experienced the acceleration and felt the vibration that shook him so hard. He described it as a sensory overload. He was nervous but then he focused back on his mission, gained more confidence and finished his mission. I talked to other astronauts and fighter pilots. By focusing on their mission, they gained back the control of their state and remained calm even when they were in a dangerous situation. I also talked to hollywood actors. They used their thoughts to produce different states.

What Drives Your Focus

Your focus is driven by your questions and interpretations. If you ask why you can never lose weight, your focus might be that you are fat. Then you continue to be fat. If you ask how you can be fitter and more toned, your focus might be eating healthier and doing more exercise. You might then come up with your meal plan and exercise program.

Your interpretation directs your focus. When you broke up with your partner, your interpretation might be that you broke up because you were not good enough, or that men are bad. On another hand, your interpretation might be that you learnt so much about yourself and what you wanted in a man. Breaking up allowed you to have a better relationship with a better person. How big a difference will these interpretations have on your next relationship?

What Magnifies Your Focus

Your sense increases or decreases your experience. You are in a different state when you change the way you see, hear or feel. Try the following suggestions; notice what turns you on or off and then use them to your advantage. If seeing increases the intensity of your experience, see things differently: movie vs still frames, big vs small, colour vs black & white, close vs far, or bright vs dark.

If hearing is the most important, hear things differently: loud vs quiet, fast vs slow, high vs low tone, saying vs hearing, regular vs irregular, or one direction vs multi directions. If you prefer to feel, feel differently: heavy vs light, hot vs cold, tension or relaxation, deep breath or shallow breath, rough vs smooth, high vs low pressure, or one pressure point vs multiple places.

Change Your State by Changing Your Focus

Your state changes when you change what you focus on, how you question things, how you interpret things and how you experience things through your senses. Your focus is your choice. Here are examples.

Choice #1	Choice #2
Failure	Success
Fear	Faith
Hatred	Love
Mistake	Lesson
Problem	Solution
Obstacle	Opportunity

2. The Physiology Expert

Change your state by changing your physiology. Every state has a specific physiology linked to it. If I tell you that there is a depressed person in room A and an excited person in room B, can you guess their facial expression, posture and breathing pattern?

A depressed person has a sad face expression, head down, looks down, touches their face, makes their body small, drops their shoulders and takes shallow breaths.

An excited person has an excited face, uses more facial muscle, smiles, opens mouth, head up, looks up, stretches body, lifts shoulders up, breathes heavily, moves a lot and probably jumps up and down. How do you know this? You practiced it at one point.

Change Your State by Changing Your Physiology

You can be in or out of a certain state by changing how you use your body. Think of top 5 states that you want to experience more and top 5 states that you want to experience less. How do you use your body in each state? If you want to avoid that state, do not use your body in a way that generates the state. If you want to experience more of that state, move your body in a way that allows you to be in that state.

If you want to adapt a state that you have not experienced before, find people who are great in that state and model their facial expression, the way they look, the way they use their body, the way they breathe and the way they tense their muscles. Do it persistently until you become it.

Amy Cuddy, an associate Professor at Harvard University, conducted a test in which people were asked to assume a "high power pose" and a "low power pose". Testosterone makes you feel confident. Cortisol makes you feel stressed.

After a 2-minute pose, the "high power" posers had a 20% increase in the level of testosterone while "low power" posers had a 10% decrease. The "high power" posers had a 2% decrease in the level of cortisol while "low power" posers had a 15% increase.

3. The Powerful Self Communication

Change your state by changing your communication. You unconsciously use words to communicate to yourself all the time. Your words reflect your thoughts and shape your state, which leads to your action and results. It is not only what you say but also how you say it: confusion vs total certainty, weak vs powerful, quiet vs loud, or irregular vs regular.

Imagine how you would feel and what state you would be in when you meet John, Jack and Jason. John softly advises you, "You are mistaken." Jack tells you, "You are wrong." Jason consistently yells at you, "You are lying!!!" Notice the big difference?

Change Your State by Changing Your Communication

If you want to know why you are in a particular state most of the time, look at the habitual words you use. If you want to experience more states, expand your vocabulary. If you want to change your state, change your words and the way you communicate to yourself. If your words do not serve you, get rid of them and replace with those that serve you. Expand your words for greater success. Here are examples.

From Bad to Good

From I am	To I am ....
fearful	curious
frustrated	challenged
breaking down	breaking through
nervous	excited
rejected	misunderstood

From Good to Great

From I am	To I am ....
awake	raring to go
confident	unstoppable
good	extraordinary
happy	all over the moon
ok to	cannot wait to

Kill the Monster while It is still Little

If you realise you are going to an unwanted state, immediately interrupt your undesirable state and embrace a state that you desire. The best time to handle an unwanted state is when you first begin to absorb it. It is easier to interrupt your pattern before it is fully immersed. For example, when you start feeling sad, do something unexpected such as jumping on a table, laughing out loud or doing a crazy dance. And then smile to change to a happy state.

What More Can You Experience Now?

1. Experience More Energy

You create what you expect. When you feel tired, move your body. The more you move, the more energy you are going to have. If you sit down, stand up, shake your body, lift your shoulders up, roll your shoulders, look straight, walk, jump or run. While moving your body, shout "I am more energised."

2. Experience More Happiness

It is important that you consistently feel good. When you feel good, you will attract more things to help you feel even better. Find out what triggers your happiness and experience more of it. Smile and laugh more often.

Smile in front of a mirror and laugh out loud for no reason. Find someone who smiles a lot and ask them why they smile so much. Listen to the words they use and pay attention to what they focus on. Find someone who has a great laugh and laughs a lot. Ask them to teach you how to model their laugh.

3. Better Experience at a Job Interview

You may have seen or done this prior to your interview. Many people sit down and look down at the floor, paper or phone while they are waiting for an interview. This makes them look small and puts them in a disempowering state.

Next time, go to a bathroom 5 minutes prior to your interview. Visualise yourself getting the job offer, hear people congratulating you for your success, feel as if you have already got the job and do an empowering pose. Expand your body, lift your hands up, clench fists, stand with legs stretched wide open and look up or look straight. While posing, shout with the feeling of a total certainty, "I now command myself to utilise all of my resources to do whatever it takes to get me this job."

While you are walking pass people, greet them like they are your best friends whom you know for years. When you enter an interview room, remain in an empowering state and tell yourself that "I am the best thing that they are going to experience." If you are in a disempowering state during the interview, change to an empowering state: sit up, clench fists under the table or do something that gains you power. When there is a mutual respect, the people who are most certain and have the most confidence influence others.

While knowledge, skill and experience are very important, a hidden differentiator which is overlooked by most people is value. You get far ahead when you find out what the interviewers' values are and fulfill them. Values influence decisions and activate actions. You are going to learn more about life values in chapter 11: Breathtaking View of Your World.

Going Blind in Space - Chris Hadfield

Chris is a retired astronaut who served as the commander of the International Space Station. When he did his first spacewalk, his left eye suddenly slammed shut with great pain. He could not see through his left eye. He asked himself what he could do next. He thought that was why he had 2 eyes so when one eye was shut, he could see through another eye.

He focused back on his mission and continued working. Without gravity, tears do not fall. He got a bigger and bigger ball of his tears and what was in it. It went across the bridge of his nose into his right eye. He was then completely blind in both eyes. He was alone in the dark outside a space ship.

The natural reaction was to be nervous and panic. But he asked empowering questions and came up with solutions. He remained in a normal state, focused on his tasks and completed his mission for that spacewalk. I recommend his talk on TED.

Another interesting example of his great state management was during a butterfly-split combat exercise. He blacked out while flying an F-18. He was unconscious in a single-seat airplane while the airplane was in the air. When he woke up, he thought it was a nice sleep then he soon realised what just happened. He controlled his state well and landed safely.

My State Saved My Life - Pitima Tongme

I saw the most beautiful private island in Maldives. Nothing was there except a few trees on a cotton white beach which was surrounded by clear light blue water. It was my number one breathtaking scenery. It was surreal so I swam out to the island.

I was not a strong swimmer but it was surprisingly easy to swim to the island. After an amazing rest, I put my snorkelling gear on and made my way out to the boat. The water was so clear. I saw beautiful fish and coral below me. I was excited.

As I swam into a deeper ocean, the coral was closer to me. The fish were bigger. The waves were stronger. It was extremely difficult for me to swim out. I swam and swam but I felt like I did not move at all. I was so tired and started to run out of breath. It was my first time in deep water. I did not know what was going to happen to me. I was scared to death.

I thought I was going to die by drowning, being sliced by sharp coral or being eaten by these huge fish around me. I closed my eyes because the most beautiful surroundings had turned into the most horrify ones. I saw a picture of my mother. She is my why. So I told myself, "I must live. I must take care of my mother." Another thought was that "I just learnt from the best coaches. I have a message that helps people improving the quality of their lives. I must live to tell these strategies."

I interrupted my pattern by thinking of a movie called Pearl Harbour. As Rafe's plane was sinking into the sea, he saw a picture of his girlfriend, Evelyn. It gave him strength. He swam out and survived. I used to think this was so dramatic and no one would do that. I then laughed because I was doing it.

My focus was to live for my mother and people who can benefit from my message. I stopped swimming, looked up, figured out why it was so difficult to swim, and found a better way to swim to the boat. I found out that I swam 90 degrees against the big waves on my way out. Hence, I hardly moved. My strategy was to swim 45 degrees against the current and then swam 135 degrees back to the boat.

I did a power pose, visualised myself stepping on that boat and shouted, "I now command myself to do whatever it takes to get me to that boat. I am absolutely going to step on that boat." I generated an intense feeling of me getting on that boat. I repeated the process for a few times until I was ready. I then swam and finally stepped on that boat.

I began to write this book since then because it is one of the two reasons I survived. I sincerely hope you find the strategies in this book useful to you.

BONUS: Success Map™

Your states from this chapter are important components of Success Map™. To complete the life-changing map you must also read chapters 3, 5 and 6. Have an instant access to Success Map™ at
www.BeTheUnstoppableYou.com/BookVIP

Chapter 5
Essential Actions
5 Steps to Turn Your Dreams into Your Reality

*"Success is not measured by
what you do compared to what others do,
it is measured by what you do with the ability God gave you."*
Zig Ziglar

People do not live their dream life for many reasons. Something stops them and they do not know how to move forward. They do not have compelling visions. They do not know how to master an empowering state. They do not know what to do to achieve their goals.

You are more advanced than many people. You know what stops you and how to move forward by using the **Escape the Wheel of Your Demons™** in chapter 1: Victor of Your Destiny and the **Awaken the Hero Within You™** in chapter 2: Remarkable Breakthrough. You have compelling goals by using the **Pyramid of Life™** and the **SMARTER Goal™** in chapter 3: Irresistible Life Design. You learnt how to master your state in chapter 4: Instant State Transformation.

The next important step to success is taking a massive determined action. You are going to learn the **5 Steps to Success™** which empowers you achieve your goal faster, easier and more efficient. You are going to discover strategies and study inspiring stories from ordinary people who have achieved extraordinary success.

This gives you a confidence to know that, regardless of your background, you can succeed when you take action. Your dream is waiting for you, to claim what is yours. Go after it. It is the only way to know what greatness you can achieve. I challenge you to make your life a masterpiece by taking a massive determined action to achieve your biggest dream.

5 Steps to Success™

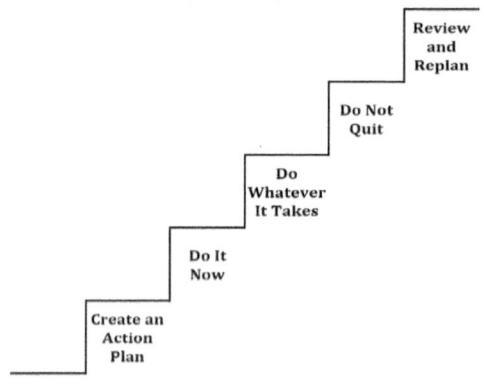

It is easier to get to where you want to be when you have a plan. Your plan is like a GPS in your car guiding you how to get to your destiny. Now is the time to do whatever it takes. Whatever you do, do not quit. Review your progress and re-examine your approach regularly. Stick with your goal but be flexible with your plan. Change to a better approach when you discover a new way that gets you to your goal faster and easier in a more enjoyable way.

1. Create an Action Plan

> *"Give me six hours to chop down a tree and*
> *I will spend the first four sharpening the axe."*
> *Abraham Lincoln*

You know where you are and where you want to go. You bridge the gap by creating a plan. Start with your ultimate result and work backwards, step by step, until you find something you can do today to move you closer to your ultimate goal.

What is your plan of actions for this year, this month, this week and today? How can you get the required resources such as money, knowledge, tools or people? You learnt how to unleash unconscious unlimited resources in chapter 2: Remarkable Breakthrough. Write down the plan.

Success Leaves Clues

> *"It is said that a wise person learns from his mistakes.*
> *A wiser one learns from others' mistakes.*
> *But the wisest person of all learns from others' successes."*
> *John C. Maxwell*

The easiest, fastest and most efficient way to achieving your goals is to find role models, coaches or mentors who continuously achieve what you want to accomplish. Success is science. If they have attained it several times for several years, they must have a formula.

When you apply the exact formula, you will have the same result. Identify and write down the names of top three to five role models who have already accomplished what you desire, approach them and learn from their success and lessons during challenging times.

You save time, money and energy by modelling their beliefs systems, physiological movements, emotional controls, question patterns, skills, tools, strategies and reasons behind their actions. You are going to learn how to find, connect and retain these successful people in chapter 6: Legendary Mastermind.

The Miraculous Faith

When a student is ready, a teacher always shows up. When I was ready to take my life to the next level, I met and learnt from Tony Robbins. My life has been phenomenally improved. When I needed to memorise for the most important exam, the UK Citizenship test, I became friends with a USA memory champion. I took 2 minutes to pass with 100%. When I was ready for a promotion, I met an executive director who later became my mentor at JPMorgan. I got the promotion.

When you meet your role models, maximise every second to listen and learn. When you are unclear, ask questions to understand but do not argue. When they tell you to do something, do not give them your excuses why you cannot do. Instead, ask them the best way to achieve it. Do it even though it sounds insane to you. They know more than you. They gave you a favour by guiding you. If you do not like the end result after doing it 10 times, take the best part out of your experience and become a better person.

If you have not had a chance to meet them yet, write down what makes them successful. Now close your eyes and imagine you are asking them what the best way to accomplish your goal. What are their answers? What do they want you to know? Write their names and their answers. Close your eyes and do the exercise now.

2. Do It Now

"What is not started will never get finished."
Johann Wolfgang Von Goethe

Great dreams are not given. They have to be earned. If you want your dream to become your reality, you cannot just dream about it. You have to take massive determined actions. If you do anything less than your best, you indirectly insult your capability. Do your best in everything you do. You deserve your best.

People do not live the life of their dreams because they fail to begin their journey. You have a choice to live with your excuses or get the results that you desire. Can you think of someone who has already achieved what you want?

Do they have more time than 24 hours? No. They just have better strategies to get more resources and manage them more efficiently. Did all entrepreneurs have a lot of money when they started their business? No. They raised money from people who could benefit from their products.

Reasons or Results

What are your reasons for not doing it: "I do not have time or money. I do not have knowledge, experience or skills."? If you are employed, does your CEO have more skill, knowledge and experience in the area that you are great at? No.

They leverage other people's skill, knowledge, experience, tool, strategy, network and everything else that they can leverage. They assign, monitor and measure the results from what they leverage effectively. You can learn these strategies from books or experts who have already done what you want to achieve.

The difference between people who live their dream life and people who wish they could is how they interpret a challenge and act upon it. The following table shows how people, who wish they could live their dream, interpret and act.

Excuse	Action
I do not know how to do that	I stop
I do not have that	I stop
I am not like that	I stop

The following table shows how people, who live the life of their dream, interpret and act.

Opportunity	Agenda
I do not know how to do "A"	To expand my knowledge on how to do "A"
I do not have "B"	To create or acquire more of "B"
I am not like "C"	To develop a character trait and become more of "C"

You are gifted but have you used your gifts to get what you want? Life will not give you more until you have done something great with what you already have. Use your gifts.

The Upgraded Version of You

"To give anything less than your best, is to sacrifice the gift."
Steve Prefontaine

When you do not accomplish something, it is rarely about your true potential. It is more about your belief towards who you can become. You have more capability than you think. If someone can do something, you can do it too.

I visited an elephant sanctuary where a wild baby elephant was chained up in Ayutthaya. I saw he was trying to break the medium size chain but he could not. He tried and tried. Later, he gave up. Years later, I visited that place again.

The baby elephant had grown up to a much bigger size. Sadly, he was still chained by a similar size chain as he had when he was younger. He could break the chain in a heartbeat but he did not try so he was forever trapped in that chain.

The lesson here is not to measure your current potential and capacity based on your past experience and capability because you are not the same person. You have grown to become a much better person with more capability. Learn from your experience and try again in a different way.

Regret or Pride

"You do not have to be great to start,
but you have to start to be great."
Zig Ziglar

Twenty years from now, you will be more disappointed by the things that you have not done than by the things you did. When the time comes, do not look at your grey hair in the mirror and ask yourself, "What the hell have I been doing? This is not my dream. This is not the life that I want. I should have done that thing a long time ago when I had the chance."

What is better than the combination of "I wish", "I should", "I would" and "I could" is "I did". Now is the perfect time to do it. You are never too young or too old to make your dreams come true. Here is a list of people and the age when started their mission.

Age	People	Founder of
20	Bill Gates	Microsoft
20	Mark Zuckerberg	Facebook
21	Steve Jobs	Apple
25	Larry Page	Google
31	J.K. Rowling	Harry Potter
45	Mary Ash	Mary Kay
52	Ray Kroc	McDonald's
62	Colonel Sanders	KFC franchise

Do Not Overthink

*"I think and think for months and years.
Ninety-nine times, the conclusion is false."*
Albert Einstein

Overthinking kills dreams. Doing is easier than overthinking. Early signs of over thinking are when you come up with excuses why you cannot or should not do, or when you try to resolve a problem that does not even exist. Can you recall this situation? You wondered with "what if....? what if....? what if....?" After you did it, you thought, "Oh, it was actually easier than I thought."

Do not try to predict the outcome or be concerned about your competition's performance. The best result comes when you detach yourself of expectation, do your very best and fully enjoy the experience. Do not give meaning to anything that does not contribute to success. Do it in spite of fear, worry, discomfort or inconvenience. Do it no matter what.

The Fire Walker - Pitima Tongme

I went to Tony Robbins's "Unleash the Power Within" event. I prepared myself to walk across a bed of hot coals at the end of the day. I learnt a certain mindset, verbal syntax, physiological move, focus point and so on. I then went to the fire bed for my first fire walk.

I was the first person in line to walk across the fire bed between 1,200 and 2,000 degrees Fahrenheit. Staffs added more red hot burning coals on the bed. The bed was on fire. I could see the red flames and smell the burning. When they gave me the signal that I could walk, I just walked like normal. I was too excited and eager to walk. I did not realise I was walking on the fire.

I did not feel the heat. My feet were fine. The staff member, who rinsed the coals out of my feet, told me I did it wrong. He said I forgot to apply the verbal syntax, physiological move and focus point before and during my walk.

So I asked if I could do it again. The staff added more burning coals. I applied what I learnt and walked. My feet were still fine. I could feel a little heat this time. I learnt that the best approach is to just do it -- do not overthink or overdo. My thought about my first fire walk was that it was just like a normal walk. My second one was that I was about to walk on fire.

Do not attempt to do this on your own. The exercise was conducted by professional teams at Tony Robbins's event. If you want to try, I recommend that you go to his event. Your life will never be the same again.

Just Do It Now

*"You do not have to see the whole staircase,
just take the first step."*
Martin Luther King

You do not need to understand everything to do anything. You do not need to know how to get to a different city before you drive. You do not need to know how electricity works to turn the light on or off. This principle applies to every area in your life. You can do anything with a little information. The key is to do it now.

"Do what you can, with what you have, where you are."
Theodore Roosevelt

The greatest defeat is giving up without trying. Now is the perfect time to start with what you have because tomorrow is not guaranteed. There is no try, no start and no end. It is "do" or "do not". Now is the right time to make your dreams become your reality.

The action activator, which switches the "do" and "do not" button on or off, is your life values. You are going to learn more about life values in chapter 11: Breathtaking View of Your World. Before then, the next most powerful thing is a simple shift.

A simple shift in your mindset helps you do or not do things. The shift is how you identify your identity. Let us assume that you just recently stopped smoking. If you identity yourself as a smoker who just quit smoking and your friend offers you a cigarette, how tempted are you to take the cigarette?

Let us imagine again that you completely change your identity. You now identify yourself as a non-smoker. You will not take the cigarette because it is not who you are. If you are a non-smoker, you do not smoke.

Unknown Opportunity

> *"Opportunity does not make appointments,*
> *you have to be ready when it arrives."*
> Tim Fargo

Things are happening everywhere. This creates an unknown opportunity. Be prepared for your opportunity, be aware of things around you and be able to spot an opportunity. When you have an opportunity, do not wait for a perfect moment. Act on it immediately like you have only one shot.

Every moment is perfect when you still have the chance. Nothing kills an opportunity more than waiting. Never allow waiting to become a habit. You and your time are too valuable to waste. If you wait, you will regret the chances that you did not take. That moment is often your last. If there is another chance, grab it and make the most out of it too.

You are not guaranteed to have the same moment again. Say "yes" to any opportunities which moves you closer to your goals even though you do not know how to achieve them. Accept the opportunity first then figure out how to do it. Do not just wait for an opportunity, create it too.

Ray Kroc was a salesman of milkshake mixers. When he received a large order from a small restaurant, he visited it. It was the busiest restaurant he had ever seen. He proposed to open a chain of these restaurants. The McDonald brothers agreed. The restaurants became even more successful. Ray then brought out the McDonald Brothers and expanded McDonald's worldwide.

Howard Schultz managed a sales force for a kitchenware company. He noticed that a small retailer placed an unusually large order for a certain type of coffee maker. He visited Starbucks and invested a year to convince them to hire him. He went to Italy for a business trip and saw the popularity of a coffee house.

Howard convinced his manager to set one up in Seattle. It was successful. He wanted to expand. His management turned him down as they viewed Starbucks as a Retailer, not a restaurant.

He resigned and set up his own coffee shop. After he raised enough capital, he bought Starbucks and expanded it worldwide.

3. Do Whatever It Takes

Expand Your Identity

"When you cannot, you must. When you must, you can."
Tony Robbins

You may not get what you want but you get your standards. You may not get your "should" but you get your "must". You always find a way and make a way to live as who you believe you are. It is time to raise a new standard, make your new standard as your "must", make your "must" as your new identity and own that identity every day. Everything you do must reflect your new identity. When you fully live your new identity, you will do whatever it takes to maintain it.

The Power of Identity - Dan Millman

From the Peaceful Warrior movie which was inspired by true events, Dan Millman was a famous gymnast who dreamed of winning a National Championship competition. He had an accident which caused his right femur bone to shatter. A metal bar was placed in his leg to maintain its integrity. He could not walk properly.

As a result, his gymnastic coach believed that Dan could not compete in the National competition and removed him from the team. Dan was hurt so he quit. He eventually remembered his identity as a gymnast. He soon restored his health, strength and gymnastic skills. After showing his true talents to his coach, he was accepted back to the team. He competed in the national competition. He and his Berkeley Gymnastics Team won their first National title.

Create Better Habits

> *"Ordinary things done consistently produce extra-ordinary results."*
> Keith Cunningham

Your new standard does not have to be an unachievable one but it should produce a better habit. You improve the quality of your life when you change your habit for a better one. For example, why don't you change from eating fatty food to running at least an hour a day? Do this for a month and notice the new result.

You have to commit to your new habit if you want a new result. Commitment does not guarantee success but lack of commitment costs you the life that you desire and deserve. It may be challenging at the beginning of the change. Keep doing it. It gets easier when you have the right momentum.

Sacrifice What You Are for What You Can Become

*"You can have anything in life if
you will sacrifice everything else for it."*
J.M. Barrie

You cannot have a new outcome if you continue doing the same thing and maintaining the same capability. It is time to grow, break out of your comfort zone, become comfortable with the unknown and take risks. Once you do, opportunity will follow you. Christopher Columbus, who discovered America, said that "You can never cross the ocean unless you have the courage to lose sight of the shore."

*"I hated every minute of training, but I said, 'Don't quit. Suffer now and live the rest of your life as a champion.' "
Muhammad Ali*

Great achievement is usually a result of great sacrifice. How badly do you want your dream? When you want your dream as badly as you want to breathe, you will do whatever it takes to get it. Be willing to do what you do not want to do. Give up the good for the great. Give up what you love if it does not contribute to the achievement of your dream. Give up your short-term needs for your ultimate goals. Sacrifice what you are for what you can become even though it means reducing your basic needs such as sleep, food or safety. Your dream is waiting for you.

The Magic Bike - Soichiro Honda

Soichiro Honda is a great example of a man who did whatever it took. He is the founder of the Honda Corporation. In 1938, He was a poor student who had a dream of designing a piston ring that he would sell to Toyota Corporation.

He went to school during the day and worked on his design at night for years. When he took it to Toyota, they rejected it. His teachers and friends told him what an idiot he was for designing such a ridiculous gadget.

He spent the next two years continuously improved the ring. Toyota finally bought it. He needed concrete to build his piston factory, but none was available because the Government was gearing up for World War II. He and his friends tried different approaches for weeks until they found a new way to manufacture concrete. He built his factory and was ready to produce his piston rings.

During the war, the United States bombed his factory and destroyed most of it. He rallied all his employees and said, "Quickly! Run outside and watch those planes. They are going to drop their fuel cans out of the sky. We need to get them, because they contain the raw materials that we cannot get in Japan but we need them for our manufacturing process." After that, an earthquake levelled his factory. He was forced to sell his piston operation to Toyota.

When the war ended, Gasoline was rare. He could not get enough gas to drive his car to buy food. He hooked a motor up to his bicycle. In that moment, the first motorized bike was created. His friends saw him ride the bike and asked him to make some for them. He soon ran out of motors.

He decided to build a new factory to manufacture motorbikes but he had no money. He wrote a letter to all bicycle shop owners in Japan, telling them that he had a solution for getting Japan moving again. His motorbike would be cheap and would help people get to where they needed to go. He asked them to invest. 18,000 bicycle shop owners received a letter. 3,000 owners invested.

He manufactured his first shipment but the motorbike was too big. Very few Japanese bought it. He stripped his motorbike down and made it much lighter and smaller. He called it The Cub, and it became an "overnight success," winning him the Emperor's Award. Today, Honda is one of the most successful companies in the world.

4. Do Not Quit

"Winners never quit and quitters never win."
Vince Lombardi

Your Winner's Spirit

You have what you want when you eliminate all options and accept only the result that you expect. Keep going until you get what you want. Determination and persistence are the insurance against failure. Let your desire for success be stronger than your willingness to accept a permanent defeat.

Why quit when you have all gifts to succeed. Do not quit even though you have slow progress or no progress at all. Progress takes time to be visible. At the end, your results always show.

> *"Men are born to succeed, not fail."*
> *Henry David Thoreau*

When you think about quitting, just tap into your winner's spirit. You are born a winner. A winner may have failed multiple times but will never quit. Can you recall a time when you were a baby and started walking? How many times did you fall? Countless. Did you quit? No.

> *"Getting knocked down in life is a given.*
> *Getting up and moving forward is a choice."*
> *Zig Ziglar*

When you fell, you got up and walked again. It was not about how many times you failed. It was about how many times you got up after your fall. Do you want proof that you have the winner spirit within you? Look at a mirror and see the evidence for yourself. You are not only able to walk but you also run!

Your Identity Myth

Every great man once failed. They failed their way to success. If you have not failed, your goal is not big enough. When you fail, failure is not your identity. It is an event. Have you ever done something stupid? Yes, we all have. Are you stupid? No, you are not. Doing a stupid thing does not mean you are stupid. This is the same as failure. When you fail, never identify yourself as a failure.

Your Permission to Succeed

> *"If I had asked people what they wanted, they would have said, 'faster horses.'"*
> Henry Ford

Have you ever thought about quitting because of disapproval? Are you waiting for someone to approve before you do something? If you are waiting for permission, stop! You do not need approval from anyone to follow your dream, not even from your parents, your spouse or your boss.

A part of your soul dies when you are silent about things that matter most to you. You have a choice to upset other people or yourself. It is okay to upset others and please yourself when it comes to your dreams. The opinion of others about your dreams is not important.

Do not let other people's voices drown your voice. After all, it is your dream. They do not see the vision that you see. Do not expect anyone to understand your vision when they have not seen it. You can tell people what you are doing but do not ask for approval. When you want to do something, do it.

Albert Einstein was not be able to speak until he was almost 4 years old. His relatives thought he was stupid. His teachers said that he would "never amount to anything". Later, he was best known for the $E = mc2$ formula.

Michael Jordon was cut from his high school basketball team. His teacher told him, "You can't slam no ball." He locked himself in his room and cried. Later, he played the summer Olympics and won many games.

The Beatles were rejected by Decca Records and were told, "Guitar groups are on the way out" and "The Beatles have no future in show business." Later, they became a famous band.

Colonel Sanders, aged 62, found the franchise of Kentucky Fried Chicken, KFC, after he had 1,009 rejections.

Great Ideas that Almost Lost - Pitima Tongme

I had a vision to create a great global community at work to improve a certain area. Many people believed in my vision and wanted to get involved. Before I implemented it, I told an executive director who was involved in that area. He did not tolerate me for a second. He told me to go away and told my manager that I should not speak to him again.

I went to him to apologise a few days later because I did not want to upset anyone. He told me not to talk to him and carelessly walked away. When people knew about this, they no longer wanted to get involved because they did not want any problems.

My mentor, a managing director, advised that I should do it when I believed that it would create a massive positive impact to the organisation. Later on that day, I saw below quote.

> *"I would rather ask for forgiveness than permission."*
> *Richard Branson*

I found out that an executive director, from another team, did a similar thing so I got involved. The previous executive director came to me a few days later. He wanted me to partner with him to implement my previous idea. There were about 40 volunteers across technology and business teams joining us globally every week. We had improved our workplace in many ways.

I was invited by the Chief Information Officer, CIO, to educate him and his Chief Technology Officers, CTO, in the weekly CTO meeting. I educated the managing directors about initiatives that I implemented. I received many emails from the CIO and CTOs saying I had created great initiatives and they were impressed. My colleagues kept thanking me for the opportunities which I provided them to succeed even more.

Your Success at the End of Your Challenge

"It always seems impossible until it is done."
Nelson Mandela

Do not let emotional or physical challenges stop you. Your struggle is your greatest success in learning. Keep pursuing your goal even though you feel the pain physically or emotionally. Go through the pain. Pain is temporary. Once the pain has gone, what is left is your success.

I had a major accident which temporarily disabled me from using my legs and one of my arms. I had to lie on a bed and not attend classes. I learnt by myself at home. After several painful physiotherapy sessions, I could walk and use my arms again. I went back to school and maintained the highest grade in my class for 6 consecutive semesters.

Morris Goodman was left completely paralysed after his plane crash. His doctor advised that he would not be able to move, speak, drink or even breathe again without a machine. The doctor was not sure if he would survive the night after the crash. He was determined and believed that he could be back to normal again. 8 months later, he walked out of the hospital by himself with no medical aid.

Your Opportunity in Disguise

*"I am not discouraged, because
every wrong attempt discarded is another step forward."
Thomas Edison*

Your failure opens a door to an opportunity that has been waiting for you. When you close the door to fear behind you, the door to faith will open right in front of you. Successful people do not use the word, "failure". They call it, "lesson". Learn the lessons from your unexpected outcomes and focus on current opportunities. When you persist in finding an opportunity, the wall will turn into a door.

Walt Disney was fired from a newspaper. His manager told him that he lacked imagination and had no original ideas. His brother helped him to get a job at a studio where he met cartoonists. Later, Walt Disney and Disney Land were born.

Oprah Winfrey was fired from her job as a television reporter. Her manger told her that she was unfit for television. She set up her own show, "Oprah Winfrey Show". This show became the highest-rated program of its kind in history.

Your Victory is Near

*"No one is ever defeated until
defeat has been accepted as a reality."*
Bruce Lee

Do not accept a temporary defeat as a permanent one. Defeat is temporary. Giving up is permanent. Whatever you do, do not give up. When you had the flu, you could not breathe through your nose. Did you give up breathing or did you try different things such as taking medicine, blowing your nose and breathing via your mouth? Let your desire for success be as strong as your need to breathe.

Many people are afraid of failure because they have a false reference that failure is a big thing. Have you ever questioned that reference? How far can you really fall? To the ground on which you spend most time? Do not be nervous about falling because you can rise higher.

Many people failed because they did not realise how close they were to success when they gave up. When your outcome is not what you expect, learn from it and use it as an inspiration to try again in a different way. When you face the most challenge, your victory is close.

When you think things are falling apart, it is when they start falling into place. When your world seems to be breaking down, it is an illusion of you breaking through. When you achieve the most challenging goal, your breakthrough is the most memorable one.

Three Feet from Gold

Darby and his uncle discovered a mine full of gold. The first car of ore was mined and shipped to a smelter. The returns proved that they had one of the richest mines in Colorado. So they kept drilling until the vein of gold ore disappeared. They thought the gold was no longer there so they quit and sold the machine to a junk man for few hundred dollars.

The junk man called in a mining engineer to look at the mine and do a little calculating. His calculations showed that the vein could be found just three feet from where the Darby had stopped drilling. That was exactly where it was found. The junk man took millions of dollars in ore from the mine.

5. Review and Replan

"Feedback is the breakfast of champions."
Ben Blanchard and Spencer Johnson

When you set a timeline to regularly review your progress, you know how far you have come and how near you are to what you are reaching out for. Your review reveals what works and what does not work. Discard what does not work and put more resources into what works.

> *"Change is the law of life."*
> *John F. Kennedy*

Do not be insane by doing the same thing and expecting a different result. Practice does not make perfect. Practice makes permanent. Continuous improvement makes it better.

> *"To improve is to change.*
> *To be perfect is to change often."*
> *Winston Churchill*

When your plan does not work, use your lesson to create a new plan. To get a better result, use a better approach. Change your plan when you discover a better tool, strategy and resource. Even though Tiger Woods is the best golfer, he continuously changed his swing to get better results.

Give Up the Good for the Great - Sylvester Stallone

Sylvester Stallone, Rocky, is an inspiring person. I admire him and his determination. When he was young, he wanted to be in the movie business. He went to agencies in New York more than 15,000 times. They rejected him and said there was no place for him in the movie industry and he would never be a star.

He was broke but he refused to get a job. He knew if he got a job and got used to it, he would feel okay about his life. He would lose his hunger. His dream would disappear. So he refused to get a job.

He went to a library to get warm and got inspired by a book. He wrote "Paradise Alley" and sold it for $100. He was still broke so he sold his wife's jewellery. That was the end of their relationship.

He loved his dog, but he and his dog starved. So he went to a store and tried to sell his dog for $50. A stranger bargained. He sold his best friend for $25. He ran away and cried.

He watched the Muhammad Ali and Chuck Wepner fight 2 weeks later. He was inspired by Wepner who kept getting knocked down in the fight but also kept coming back for more. After the fight, he spent the next 20 hours straight writing the Rocky movie. He tried to sell it to agencies. All agencies refused, except one group of people.

They offered him $125,000 for the script. Everything went well until he said he wanted to star in it; they wanted Ryan O'Neal to star. Even though he was starving, he refused to sell the script. They came back and offered $250,000 then $325,000 for just the script. He refused to sell at any price unless he starred in it. They finally offered him $35,000 and let him star in it. He sold the script.

He went to the liquor store and waited for 3 days. He wanted to buy his dog back. He offered $100, $500 and $1,000 but the new owner refused to sell. Finally, he offered $15,000 and a part in the Rocky movie. The owner accepted. He had his dog back. The dog in the movie was his real dog.

Whatever It Takes - Pitima Tongme

*"If we did all the things we are capable of,
we would literally astound ourselves."*
Thomas Edison

My dream was to work in a leading investment bank in London. After finishing my Master's Degree in IT, I applied for a position in many banks in London. I did not get any interviews from banks. I got an offer at the Guardian Media Group in Berkshire.

I found out about the Highly Skilled Migrant Program, HSMP. This visa would allow me to work in the UK longer. The challenge was that I had to earn 12 months' salary within 9 months. I had only 4 months to accomplish this or my visa would expire.

I did whatever it took to increase my income because the amount was needed to be on my payslip as my earning evidence for the HSMP visa. I asked for a pay raise. My salary was 25% increased. I did not like having a long commute to work but I volunteered to travel and work at different locations so that my expenses could be added to my pay slip. It took me 2 more hours to commute every day.

After my IT work, I worked as a waitress at a restaurant until midnight. I worked there for about a week. They refused to pay me. I then worked in a night club instead of that job. I collected dirty glasses until 2 AM in my Hugo Boss clothes.

My mother and friends kept telling me to go back to Bangkok. My ex-boyfriend told me to choose between working there and being with him. They did not see the vision that I saw. Every time I collected a glass, it was not about collecting the glass. I pictured myself working at JPMorgan in London.

I broke up with the first guy I ever loved. I cried all day and night when I was alone. It was not easy to work from 9 AM - 2 AM with only 4 hours sleep after a major breakup. I was challenged both physically, emotionally and mentally.

I luckily got myself a new night-time job as an IT supervisor. They paid me twice what the night club did. I worked until midnight. After work, I walked to the town centre. I was chased by a group of men. I went to the police. They gave me an alarm. When I was chased the following night, I activated the alarm but no one opened the door to help me.

I sometimes took a taxi home but the taxi cost was twice what I earned at the night job. So I sometimes ran from the gang in a dark long road at midnight. I slept at 2 AM and woke up at 7 AM. I worked like that for a few weeks, earned enough points for my visa and applied for it.

I got my HSMP visa. JPMorgan then offered me an opportunity in the very competitive Elite Graduate Program in Technology for high-calibre people. I excelled there and got a promotion. I was invited by the Chief Information Officer to educate him and his Chief Technology Officers, managing directors, in the weekly CTO meeting.

At the end of my HSMP visa, I could apply for a permanent visa if I passed an exam. I like this kind of detailed test less than a mathematic one. I luckily became a friend of Ron, the two time USA memory champion.

Ron privately taught me how to prepare for my test about a week prior to the test. People had to achieve 75 percent within 45 minutes. An hour before the real exam, I took an official practice test. I spent less than 2 minutes and achieved 100%. I took a similar amount of time during the real test and passed the exam.

After receiving the permanent visa, I am now proud to announce that I am a British citizen and hold a UK passport. I am a multi-millionaire in Thailand. I socialise with Visionary Entrepreneurs, Oscars Award Winners, Hollywood Producers, Grammy Award Winners, World Champions and NASA Moonwalkers. I travel to my dream places around the world. This was beyond my wildest dreams when I was almost homeless in poverty in Bangkok. When you refuse to give up, you can live your ultimate dream.

BONUS: Time Mastery System™

"Lost time is never found again."
Benjamin Franklin

Imagine. There is a bank that credits your account each morning with £86,400. But it deletes whatever part of the amount you had failed to use during the day. What would you do? Draw out every penny. Each one of us has such a bank. It is called, "Time".

Every morning it credits you with 86,400 seconds. Every night it writes off as lost whatever of this you have failed to use wisely. If you fail to use the day's deposits, the loss is yours. Do you use every second wisely?

To realise the value of one minute, ask a person who just missed a train. To realise the value of one second, ask a person who just avoided an accident. To realise the value of one millisecond, ask a person who won a silver medal at the Olympics. Time waits for no one. You must maximise every moment. When you master your time, you master your life.

> *"We always have time enough, if we will but use it aright."*
> Johann Wolfgang Von Gorthe

How many times have you heard or spoken this phrase, "If only I could add more hours to my day"? In today's fast-paced world, having too much to do in too little time is a common challenge. Although you are overwhelmed and exhausted with multi-tasking, your to-do list keeps growing longer and you feel like you are a step behind.

What do you use your time for? On the left column, write the main activities that you spend most of your time doing in a day.

Main Activities	Major Goals

On the right column, write down your top 3 goals for this year. Link each activity to the goal that it massively contributes to greater success. How much do your main activities move you closer to your main goal? Congratulations if your main activities massively contribute to the achievement of your biggest goals. If not, are you overwhelmed doing the wrong things?

> "One of the very worst uses of time is to do something very well that need not to be done at all."
> Brian Tracy

Your life does not have to be this way. It is time to take back the control of your time and your life by applying the following Time Mastery System™ to maximise your time for peak performance:

- List things that need to be done. If today were your last day, what would be the most important thing to be done?
- Prioritise each item using Importance (1-3) and Urgency (1-3), IU method. Focus on the Highest Importance and the Highest Urgency.
- Schedule your top prioritised items.
- Only do your best at what you are great at and decide on important things that need your ultimate decision.
- Delegate or outsource the rest to specialists.
- Make your daily "10 Before 10" list before you go to bed. It is the list of 10 most important things that you commit to accomplish before 10 AM the next morning. They are 10 things that contribute to 90% of success.

- Do your "10 Before 10" list, which is ordered by the above IU method, without any distractions or procrastination.
- Reward yourself when you accomplish your "10 Before 10" list.
- Implement a process to eliminate or automate work.
- Find a way to continuously improve yourself, your product, service, technology, process or people.

For the latest version, visit
www.BeTheUnstoppableYou.com/Time-Management-Mastery

BONUS: Success Map™

Your actions from this chapter are important elements of Success Map™. To complete the life-changing map you must also read chapters 3, 4 and 6. Have an instant access to Success Map™ at
www.BeTheUnstoppableYou.com/BookVIP

Chapter 6
Legendary Mastermind
How to Win and Influence Almost Anyone

"If I have seen further it is by standing on the shoulders of giants."
Isaac Newton

No great thing has been accomplished by a single person without a team behind that person. Your mastermind is an express way to more success. When you surround yourself with more successful people, you will become even more successful.

You learnt how important it is to have mentors and successful people around you in previous chapters. You are going to learn how to find, attract and retain them in this chapter. You will also learn how to become a highly likeable person who quickly connects with others at a deeper level.

Many people ask me how I met NASA moonwalkers, top visionary entrepreneurs, world champions, Grammy award winners and Oscar award winners, and how I remain in contact with some of them. I reveal my secrets in this chapter.

You are going to learn:
- 4 Steps for Mastering Your Success Group

- 5 Secrets for the Most Captivating Conversation
- 3 Character Traits of a Highly Likable Person
- 3 Magic Bonds for Any Personalities, Perspectives and Styles

Why You Have a Success Group

- You can leverage resources such as skill, knowledge, experience and tool.
- You can have access to meet more successful people at a higher level.
- You can do business together or you can have surprise job offers.

Surprise Job Offers - Pitima Tongme

Directors who I used to work with, and vice presidents who heard about my reputation, often persuaded me to take surprise job offers without me even looking for a job. When they approached me, I did not have any experience in the roles and I did not have business knowledge in those areas. I just always did outstanding work and built an extraordinary relationship. You can have surprise job offers too when you do great work and develop a great relationship with powerful influencers.

Types of Success Groups

There are several types of success groups such as mentors, specialists and joint ventures. Mentors are people who are where you want to be and have what you want to have. Success is science. People never reach their full potential without a first class coach.

When you apply the right formula, you will have the same result. You save time, money and energy by learning from their success and lessons during challenging times. A faster way to success is to model their belief system, physiology, emotional control and question pattern, as well as acquiring their skill, tool, strategy and network.

Specialists are people who are exceptionally great at what they do. You can leverage knowledge, skill, experience, tool and strategy. Henry Ford had a row of electric push-buttons on his desk and, by pushing the right button, he could summon to his aid men who could answer any questions he had concerning the business. He surrounded himself with people who could supply the knowledge he required.

Joint ventures are people who are already offering tremendous values, generating massive sales, and who have a huge database of raving fans who are your potential clients.

When you build a spectacular relationship with them and construct a deal structure, you can create greater results, make bigger impacts and generate more residual revenue.

Famous Mastermind Groups

The Vagabonds - Henry Ford, Harvey Firestone, Warren G. Harding, Thomas Edison and Luther Burbank took a road trip each summer. They competed in tree chopping and climbing contests to allow Nature's Laboratory inspire them to new ideas. They discussed their business ventures and debated the pressing issues of the day.

The Tennis Cabinet - Theodore Roosevelt spent time with Major-General Leonard Wood, Gifford Pinchot, Bill Sewell and others. They hiked, climbed cliffs, rode horses and played tennis. They exercised their minds while working their bodies. They discussed the pressing issues of the day and planned out the best way to proceed.

The Inklings - The Lord of the Rings and other famous books were polished by The Inklings. These included great poets and writers such as CS Lewis, JRR Tolkien, Charles Williams, and Owen Barfield. They read aloud their writings and the other members offered constructive feedback.

Control Your Surrounding for Greater Success

*"You are the average of the five people
you spend the most time with."*
Jim Rohn

You become like the people who you spend the most time with. Your life is a reflection of the expectations of your peer group. If your peer group does not expect much, it is just a matter of time before you lower your expectations of yourself. If your peer group expects a lots from you, you will rise to their expectations. Therefore, it is important that you control who you are with. Surround yourself only with people who have high standards and expectations.

There are two types of people: toxic and nurturing. Toxic people complain, and blame anything for their circumstances. They talk badly about everything. They stop you from achieving your goals by affirming that your dream is impossible or you are not good enough. They drag you down to their level. You feel bad when you are around them.

Nurturing people are those who you want to become, who are optimistic, who see opportunities, who believe in their dreams, who are results-oriented, who know they can accomplish anything, and who do whatever it takes until they achieve their goals. They believe in you, help you clarify your goals, suggest action plans, keep you focused on top priorities, demand your best and bring out the best in you.

They challenge you to succeed at the next level, discover your blind spots, point out opportunities and open doors for you. They provide you with the best tools, connect you with successful people and support you to achieve your goals. You feel great by just hearing their names or being around them.

> *"Surround yourself only with people
> who are going to take you higher."*
> Oprah Winfrey

It is fun to make a list of everyone you spend time with on a regular basis: your family, friends, business partners, colleagues, neighbours and so on. Put a minus sign (-) next to toxic people and a plus sign (+) next to nurturing people.

It is necessary to avoid toxic people at all costs. Toxic people have to go. Now is the time to stop spending time with people who have (-) next to their names. If you cannot stop entirely, spend less time with them. Never listen to toxic people because they will destroy your dream. You are better off spending time alone than with people who bring you down and hold you to the ground.

It is important that you do whatever it takes to be surrounded with people who have (+) next to their names. It is about investing in quality time with quality people. It is a great idea to make another list of people who have not yet be in your circle but with whom you want to be connected, such as the experts who help you reach your goal faster and easier.

> "It is better to hang out with people better than you. Pick out associates whose behaviour is better than yours and you will drift in that direction."
> Warren Buffett

The key is to surround yourself with people who are smarter and more successful than you. If you are the smartest and the most successful person in your group, it is time to challenge yourself to a higher level and acquire a more successful group. Now, you are going to learn how to identify, find, attract and retain your success group.

4 Steps for Mastering Your Success Group

> "I absolutely believe that people, unless coached, never reach their maximum capabilities."
> Bob Narddelli

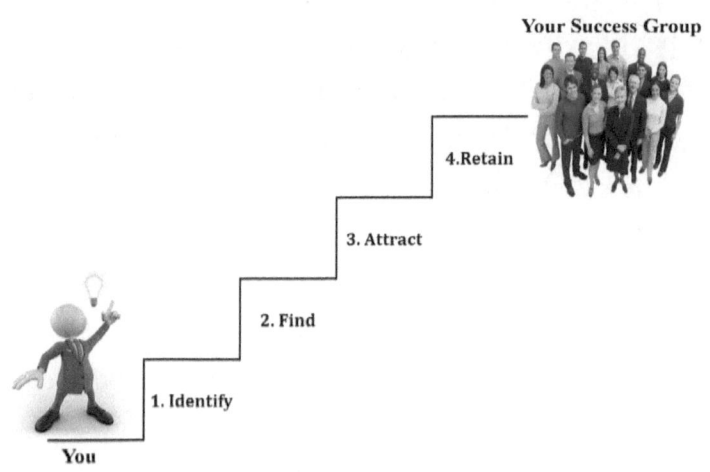

Step#1. Identify - The Success Compass

Identify people who you want to surround yourself with. Name top three to five people for each category listed above. Aim high and get the best people. The best and most influential people attract more great people.

Entering a High Performing Executive League - Pitima Tongme

I saw the Chief Technology Officer (CTO) talking to his manager, the Chief Information Officer (CIO) with whom I wanted to connect. I approached the CTO, congratulated him for being the top service provider and asked him for his feedback about major improvements that I made for his teams.

He then gave a great introduction about me to his manager who was 3 levels down from Jamie Dimon, CEO of JPMorgan. From then on, I met up with the CIO when he visited London and had a phone conversation when he was in New York. He introduced me to other directors. This was how I expanded my network and found more mentors.

Step#2. Find - The Hot Spots

The best way to find your success group is to think like them so that you are in the same place at the same time. If you have a mutual friend, gain some insights from your friend. The key is not only to be seen by your success group but also to be recognised by them through memorable interaction.

You can find them by:
- Attending their seminars or events.
- Going to charities or other events that they go to.
- Participating in specialised business conferences.
- Taking part in professional associations.
- Joining existing mastermind groups or creating ones.

Step#3. Attract - You as A Giant Magnet

> *"People do not care how much you know until they know how much you care."*
> *Mark Twain*

A Better Introduction

Start by dressing exceptionally well to represent a high value person. Even better than "Dress to impress" is "Dress for head turn and jaw dropping". When you embrace the power of beauty that arouses curiosity and interest from others, people will wonder, and be eager to find out who you are.

At the event, ask a respectable mutual friend or a person who is at a higher level to introduce you to them. It is better to have someone, who they respect, introduce you to them.

A Success Way to an Instant Attention Grabbing - Pitima Tongme

I saw the executive director, who had just promoted me, was chatting in a group of directors with whom I wanted to connect. I praised him about his help to better my performance. He told other directors about my performance and the promotion.

A couple of days later, a managing director and an executive director in the group became my mentors. I had a meeting with each of them weekly. This led to an additional mentor who later became my Chief Technology Officer. I improved massively by learning from their wisdom, success and lessons, as well as leveraging their tools and network.

Another story is about grabbing attention even though you are at a different location. Les Brown's business partner is a great friend of mine. Before I attended an event that Les was attending, I asked my friend in the US to introduce me to Les while Les was in Los Angeles and I was in London. I did not meet Les at the event. I met Les a year later. He remembered that we were supposed to have a meeting the previous year. We talked many times over two days. He gave me great insights. He runs many events worldwide.

5 Secrets for the Most Captivating Conversation

"Stop selling. Start helping."
Zig Ziglar

- **Start in a friendly way.** Pay them a sincere compliment and give them a genuine thank you. When they feel great about themselves, they feel great about you. The art of giving a compliment is to give a rare compliment.

  For example, a beautiful lady always get, "You are beautiful." All the time. A smart gentleman always gets "You are smart." A breakthrough expert always gets "You have changed my life."

Instead of paying a common compliment, find out another unique thing that will make them feel great about themselves in an even more special way. It will be even more powerful if it aligns with their values.

- **Focus on them.** Build an irresistible rapport and create an outstanding relationship with them by getting to know them. Find out about their why, their current or upcoming projects or their turning points. Ask what they want so that you can give it to them and what challenges they have so that you can offer solutions or at least connect them with experts.

- **Listen and learn when they talk.** So that you know how to add more values by offering them something which is personalised and unexpected.

- **Ask them the best way to communicate with them directly.** So that you can offer more values. Before you ask for their direct contact, ask yourself, "How can I arouse their interest and influence them to want to give me their direct contact? How can this benefit them?" Convince them that the idea is theirs. The best way to allure them into an idea is to plant it in their mind.

- **Deliver what you offer and expect nothing in return.** I love strawberries but fish prefer worms. If I go fishing, I will not bait the hook with a strawberry. Rather, I will hang a worm in front of the fish. You can get someone to do anything by giving them what they want. Find out what they want, personalise it and give it to them.

Note: Pay attention to people around them and engage them as well. They might be their influencers.

Your Pitch That Sells

"A sale is made on every call you make. Either you sell the client some stock or he sells you a reason he cannot buy. Either way, a sale is made. The only question is who is going to close? You or him?"
The Boiler Room

Successful people do not care about you initially. They get chased and approached by many people. They probably run away if you try to sell yourself when they are not yet interested. You should talk about yourself only when they ask you. It means they are interested in you. When you talk, talk with confidence, and talk about things that they can relate to.

Have the following introduction ready so that you can use it when they ask what you do:

- Who you are: your name, title and company. Make yourself unique by not using "a". You should find a way to use "the". If you are a real estate agent and you publish a book, say, "I am the real estate agent who published a book called, 'How to Sell Your House at 25% Higher Price.' "
- What you do and what results you consistently deliver. Can they get the same results too?
- Why you? What is your unique selling point?
- How you give back to the society e.g. what charity you support.
- Call for an urgent action. Give them your contact details and convince them why they should contact you immediately.

Step#4. Retain - The Irresistible VIP Space

"Try not to become a man of success, but rather try to become a man of value."
Albert Einstein

It is good when your VIPs first think of you before somebody else. It is even better when they would rather wait for you than contacting someone else. Two ways to convince your

VIPs to think that being with you is irresistible, and leaving is not an option, are consistently adding massive values more than everyone else and remaining in existence.

A Guarantee for a Long Lasting Relationship

Would you like to meet very successful people for one time reason or a lifetime? The best way to retain your success group is to add massive values that they want.

3 Steps for Adding Massive Values

- Discover what they want. It can be to solve their challenge, connect them with specific people, make them more money, promote their event, sponsor their event, support their charity or give them important information.
- Go and get it. If you do not have it, leverage from someone who has it. If it does not exist, invent it. Otherwise, use the flexible strategy in chapter 2: Awaken the Hero within You, to come up with a similar thing that they want.
- Gain their trust by giving them what you offer.

A Way to Make the Relationship Last

A good way to stay in touch is to schedule a regular meeting: weekly, biweekly or monthly. The meeting can be on phone, skype, google hangout or face to face. The meeting usually lasts for an hour for four people. During the meeting, each member shares ideas, information, opportunities and resources, as well as discussing challenges and solutions. When they suggest something, you should do it and let them know the results.

Have you considered an accountability partner? You agree to a goal and hold each other accountable for achieving that goal. You agree to call each other every week to follow up on progress. You may find the day before the meeting is your most productive day due to the time pressure.

3 Character Traits of a Highly Likable Person

"If you would win a man to your cause,
first convince him that you are his sincere friend."
Abraham Lincoln

You know what they want when they like you and open to you. Be a highly likeable person. People do not normally open up to you unless they like you. Following are the character traits of highly likeable person.

Character#1. Begin in a friendly way

"A smile is the light in your window that tells others that there is a caring, sharing person inside."
Denis Waitley

Start by smiling with a massive enthusiasm when you interact with people. A smile says, "I am glad to see you. I like you. You make me happy." A charming smile is the real smile that comes from your heart and reflects through your eyes.

How good do you feel when someone smiles at you? Did you smile back? When you smile, did you feel good? If you want someone to feel good about you, a sincere smile is a gateway.

If you have had a tough day and do not feel like smiling, use 3 state management strategies from chapter 4: Instant State Transformation. When you think of the happiest or funniest moment, you will smile naturally and instantly.

Character#2. Make them feel special

*"People do not buy for logical reasons.
They buy for emotional reasons."*
Zig Ziglar

Who do you like the most? Can you remember the whole conversation or can you remember only how you felt when you were around them? We may not remember what they say but we always remember how they make us feel, in particular a great feeling.

The Most Magical Sentence - Michael Bolton

Michael Bolton is a role model who I highly admire. He is my number one favourite singer. I love his music since I first saw his music video, the Best of Love. More importantly, I love his inspiring story and his determination to succeed. Going to his concert is a once in a lifetime experience. He is a great Grammy award winner who is so friendly. He makes people feel great when they are around him.

When I first met him, we chatted for a long time. Before we left, he said happy birthday to me in front of a camera. I met him again 10 months later. He asked me about many things which only my close friends know about me.

I was surprised when he asked about my mother in Thailand and the situation in Thailand. So I asked him how he knew that my mother was in Thailand. I thought he was guessing. But then he whispered, "I remember." That one sentence, that my role model said, has made my heart sing until now.

The WOW Comment - Dr John Demartini

Dr John Demartini, from The Secret movie, is a great teacher that inspires me. His heartfelt stories deeply touched my heart. During a conversation, he played with my hair in a friendly way and said, "I remember you from 2 years ago. You had darker hair." Wow!

I first briefly and accidently met him 2 years ago while I was walking on a street and he was getting a taxi. Yes, my hair was a bit darker on that day. I was highly surprised by the level of detail that he remembered. He has a great memory. He consistently reads over 3,000 books and teaches over 300 days a year. If you want a better life, go to his events.

Why don't you be a mood creator who makes everyone feel great just because you are around? When you make people feel as though they are at their best in your presence, they want to be around you even more.

Greet people by their names. Their names are the most magical words to them. When you say their names, you make them feel special and important. It tells them that you care to remember and it makes them feel special.

> *"There is more hunger for love and appreciation in this world than for bread."*
> Mother Teresa

People crave to be appreciated and treated in a special way. They will always remember you when you give them a genuine compliment that makes their heart sing for years. You make them feel great when you genuinely admire them or sincerely treat them like they are the most important people in the world.

Tom Brokaw tapped Donald Trump's shoulder and said, "Thanks, Donald, for what you have done for NBC (The Apprentice Program). We really appreciate it." Tom's comment made Donald thought that it was maybe the reason why everyone at NBC, as well as the public, loves and respects Tom.

You should not speak negative about anyone. Everyone is superior in some ways. So why not praise all the good you know of everyone, privately and publicly? You should not criticise or complain. Criticism wounds people's precious pride, shrinks their sense of importance and hurts their feelings. There is always a good thing in everything.

When Edward Bedford lost a million dollars for the firm by a bad buy in South America, John Rockefeller knew Bedford had done his best. So Rockefeller congratulated Bedford because Bedford had been able to save 60 percent of the money.

Character#3. Be a Great Communicator

*"When I am getting ready to reason with a man,
I spend one-third of my time thinking about
myself and what I am going to say and
two-thirds about him and what he is going to say."*
Abraham Lincoln

People are interested in people who are interested in them. Get their attention by expressing a genuine interest in them. People talk for hours and like you for it when you encourage them to talk about themselves, their accomplishments and their inspirations. Let them do a great deal of the talking. While they are talking, be a great listener and learn from their talk. It is important to pay exclusive attention to the person who is talking, and not interrupt even though you are tempted. To earn respect, you must first give it.

When you talk, you should see things from their point of view and talk in their language, in terms of what they are interested in. You touch someone's heart by talking about what they treasure most.

A night before Theodore Roosevelt expected a visitor, he stayed up late and read up on the subject in which he knew his guest was interested, so that he knew what to say no matter what his guest's background was.

The Magic Bonds for a Deeper Connection

Rapport is a magic bond that unites people and allows you to enter someone else's world. People like those who are like them or who are like how they want to be. Create rapport by having something in common: shared background, experience, beliefs, interests or friends. If you do not know what you have in common yet, start by mirroring them.

You do not give up your identity while mirroring someone. Mirroring is a way to share an experience with someone and understand them from their point of view. Mirror their posture, facial expression, eye contact, head position, body movement, placement of body parts, breathing patterns, approximately and so on. Reflect their voice: speed, volume, tempo, tone and keyword. Once the bond is connected, you can lead and persuade them from their point of view.

A Great Communication through Their Personalities

> *"A person hears only what they understand."*
> Johann Wolfgang Von Goethe

People perceive the world in different ways: visual, auditory or kinesthetic. You can enter someone's world by adapting their style.

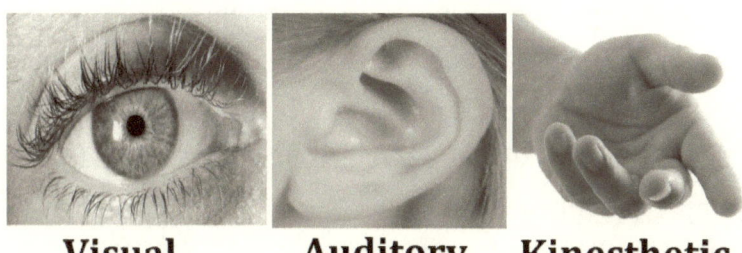

Visual **Auditory** **Kinesthetic**

Visual people look at the world through visual images. They use images to understand something. The majority of them talk fast when they are in a normal state. They also point a lot to show people something. When people are in a visual mode, they tend to look up to visualise things. They often use words like: look, see, picture, imagine, view, vision, show and clear. Examples of phrases are:
- I see your point.
- I can imagine that.
- I want you to take a look at this.

Auditory people listen carefully to what people say. They remember people and events by the words that people said. When people are in an auditory mode, they may tilt their head to lift their ear up to receive the sound better. They speak clearly. They often use words like: hear, sound, listen, tell, say, discuss, interview, speechless and tune in. Examples of phrases are:
- I hear what you are saying.
- It sounds great.
- Does it ring a bell?

Kinesthetic people understand best while touching and moving. They do things slowly. They tend to speak slower and take longer pauses when they are in a normal state. They often use words like: handle, feel, touch, hold, catch and slip. Examples of phrases are:

- I can handle this.
- It feels right.
- I am not sure I am following you.

A Great Communication through Their Perspectives

"When you are finished changing, you are finished."
Benjamin Franklin

If you talk slowly and someone talks very fast, how easily can he get through to you? Probably not very easily. You probably annoy and ignore him. If he rushes you to talk quickly, you may think that he is rude. In contrast, if you talk very fast and he talks very slowly, you may get bored and ask him to hurry up.

You are not a solo visual, auditory or kinesthetic person. Why not adapt your style to get what you want? The following are suggestions of how to deal with different types of people.

Dealing with Visual:
Do
- Rather than just talking, show them colour coded

visual aids: pictures, diagrams, graphs or charts.
- To increase their sense: make the image moving, use more vivid colour, bring it closer, make it bigger, provide more views from different angles and so on.

Don't
- Do not speak slowly and quietly with long pauses.

Dealing with Auditory:

Do
- Rather than showing them details, speak to them clearly in a medium pace and emphasise key points by changing tonality.
- To increase their sense: make the sound moving around them, make it louder, make the rhythm more regular, make it sudden, add more bass and so on.

Don't
- Do not have other auditory distractions.

Dealing with Kinesthetic:

Do
- Rather than teaching them a theory, let them do things. Engage their physiology e.g. test drive.
- To increase their sense: add more vibration, put more weight, apply more pressure, increase the temperature and so on.

Don't
- Do not speak quickly and do not rush them.

A Great Communication through Their Channels

You make an immediate impact when you present your tailored message to suit your audience. Before you begin the conversation, think about how much they already know about the topic, and at which level of detail they need to know more, so that you give only necessary information to their favourite channel. Different people prefer to be contacted by different channels depending on their lifestyle and schedule. You should ask how to best engage them and what is the best contact detail for that channel, to get a better response.

A Question for the Best Response - Pitima Tongme

Before I became a friend of the President of a major space related company, he suggested that the best way to contact him was to call his mobile or email him. When I called, he was often on another call. So the better way was to email to schedule a call.

When I emailed his work address, it took him a few days before he responded. I guessed my email was buried with his other thousand unread work emails. So I asked for the best email to get a quicker response. He gave me his personal email address. From then, I often got a response instantly or within a couple of hours, and we have become very good friends since.

A Great Communication through Their Styles

There are 4 types of personalities: Driver, Expressive, Analytical and Amiable. Drivers focus on results, make things concise and like to direct. Expressive personalities focus on big picture, prefer examples and have things concise. Analytical people focus on details, prefer facts, love stats, desire for options and recommend only when the case is clear. Amiable characters focus on feeling, avoid conflict, need time to think and let the team make a decision.

Dealing with Drivers:
Do
- Start with what they need to know or do.
- Be direct and concise. Give an executive summary on results.

Don't
- Do not propose a long meeting, do not be ineffective and do not be indecisive.

- Do not discuss feelings or irreverent topics.

Dealing with Expressive personalities:
Do
- Start with the big picture.
- Communicate a fun, exciting, inspiring, high energy, friendly and flexible dialogue.

Don't
- Do not turn them off with detail, routine, schedules and inflexibility.
- Do not be pessimistic.

Dealing with Analytical people:
Do
- Give accurate detailed facts, charts or anything else that helps them make a better decision.
- Give options.

Don't
- Do not rush them to answer when they do not have enough information.
- Do not mess with their calendar or surprise them at the last minute.

Dealing with Amiable characters:
Do
- Slow down to their pace, be patient and be supportive.
- Let them participate.

Don't
- Do not engage or rush them to answer on the spot.
- Do not create a conflict or start an argument.

Be Ready for Your Success Group

*"Before everything else,
getting ready is the secret of success."*
Henry Ford

When you stay ready, you do not have to get ready. You are always at your best. You always know what to do and say even though an opportunity takes you by surprise. The key is to stay ready all the time. A great relationship begins when you master the following activities:
- Thermostat your environment.
- Identify and find your success groups.
- Attract and retain your success groups:
    o Come up with questions that excite them.
    o Add more personalised values.
    o Arouse their interests to give you direct contact details.
    o Sharpen your pitch.
    o Schedule regular meaningful meetings with them.
- Develop 3 character traits of a highly likable person:
    o Smile more often.
    o Be a mood creator who makes people feel great and be at their best when they are around you.

- - Be a great communicator who listens more and talks in their language in terms of what interests them.
- Build a deeper rapport by adapting your perspective to suit visual, auditory or kinesthetic preferences.
- Communicate by adapting your style to suit Driver, Expressive, Analytical and Amiable personalities.

Prioritise the Right Ones

*"Never make someone a priority when
all you are to them is an option."
Maya Angelou*

Prioritise people who continuously support you even when you are at your lowest, and who always be with you when you need help. Treasure people, who never look at their calendar when you want their time and do not take them for granted.

Do not chase or make someone a priority when they see you as an option, no matter how successful that person is or how much you want to connect with them. A great relationship is built on mutual respect.

When you become the best version of yourself and get better every day, the right people will come and stay, just by your being who you are. Be your best and attract the best people.

BONUS: Success Map™

Your mastermind from this chapter is the last component of Success Map™. To complete the life-changing map you must also read chapters 3, 4 and 5. Have an instant access to Success Map™ at

www.BeTheUnstoppableYou.com/BookVIP

PART THREE

THE PSYCHOLOGY

OF

ACCELERATING

Chapter 7
Advanced Affirmation
5 Steps to Summon the Best You

*"It is the repetition of affirmations that leads to belief.
And once that belief becomes a deep conviction,
things begin to happen."*
Muhammad Ali

Advanced Affirmation is a powerful process to reclaim your true identity and bring out the best you. You engage all your senses and attach an incredible amount of emotion while you are repeatedly saying powerful words. Advanced Affirmation empowers you in 3 ways:

1. Advanced Affirmation subconsciously summons who you are destined to be and influence your world to be as per what you intensely and constantly command.
2. Advanced Affirmation conditions your nervous system and taps into your subconscious mind to automatically attract and do things that help you achieve your goal faster and easier than you ever imagined.
3. Advanced Affirmation sends a strong command to your brain to register that your intention is very important. Your Reticular Activating System will be reinforced to recognise available resources that have always been there for you but that you did not notice previously.

5 Steps to Summon the Best You

Your thoughts and words are the declarations of who you believe you are and how the world should be. You recondition yourself by using Advance Affirmation.

Advance Affirmation

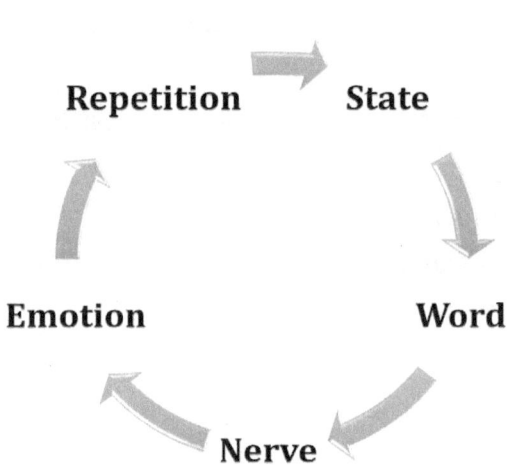

1. Put Yourself in an Empowering State

Put yourself in an empowering state before you begin your affirmation process. You learnt how to instantly put yourself in any state in chapter 4: Instant State Transformation. For example, if you want to be more confident, lift your whole body up and push your shoulders back. If you want to be in the peak state or have more energy, listen to your favourite song and jump along for 3-5 minutes.

2. Declare Powerful and Inspiring Words

You are what you repeatedly think and say. You create what you expect. Your thoughts and words reflect on who you believe you are and how the world should be. Your thoughts and words subconsciously shape your life and draw circumstances to you. If you want a better life, monitor your thoughts, think only positive things and say only empowering words. You will see examples of powerful affirmations at the end of step 5.

Here are a few guidelines for creating your affirmations:
- Start with "I am"
- Avoid using the word "not"
- Use positive and powerful words
- State in a present sense
- Use rhythm

3. Engage All Your Nerves

Start by moving your entire body: face muscles, shoulders, arms, hands and legs. Then say your affirmation out loud. For even more powerful results, declare it while making eye contact with yourself in the mirror and emphasise each word.

When you close your eyes, see yourself as who you wish to become. If you are imagining an object, grab it and feel it. If there was someone with you when you achieved your goals, what would they say? Hear their words of encouragement and congratulation. If there is another sound, what do you hear? If you are tasting something, what does it taste like?

4. Attach Massive Emotional Intensity and Certainty

Attach a massive emotional intensity and have an absolute conviction that your affirmation is your identity while saying it at the top of your lungs. Generate the incredible feeling of burning desire, faith, joy, happiness, fulfillment, excitement, love and gratitude to suit each affirmation. It is important that you believe what you say and be able to feel it.

5. Repeat It Again and Again

Give yourself a gift by doing advanced affirmation at least twice a day: when you wake up and before you go to bed. Declare each affirmation at least ten times so that it gets stuck in your head. Each time, say it louder, attach more emotional intensity and engage more senses.

Imagine you have to continuously declare your identity ten times to a stranger who does not believe who you say you are. How would the level of your emotional and physical intensity increase each time you declare? At the end of this chapter, you are going to learn how Alec Baldwin conditions himself from a victim to a victor in a movie called *The Edge*.

Here are examples of powerful affirmations:

Area	Affirmation
Health and Fitness	* Every day and every way I am stronger and stronger. * I am grateful for having great health. * Thank you for my healing.
Personal Development	* Every day and every way, I am better and better. * I am guided in every way. All I need is within me now. * I am the best I can possibly be.
Relationship	* As I love myself, I am all I ever need. * I am in a passionate relationship with my soul mate. * I am blessed with a fantastic family and friends.
Business or Career	* I am successful in all that I do. * I am worthy. Everyone wants to do business with me. * I am excited watching orders pouring in for my new product.
Wealth	* I am a money magnet. * I am an excellent receiver of wealth and abundance. * I am a brilliant money manager.
Lifestyle	* I love my life. * I am living in the house of my dreams. * I am thrilled as I am driving my Ferrari 458 Spider.
Contribution	* I am leaving a legacy that lives longer than my life. * I am a generous giver. * I am adding values to other people's lives.

Now, take a few minutes to create your own affirmations. Refer to your dream list in chapter 3: Irresistible Life Design.

For the next 3 months, schedule the Advanced Affirmation at least 10 minutes a day so that it becomes your new habit. Research from NASA shows that it takes about 21-30 days to re-program your brain. So your first 30 days will be about re-wiring your nerves. Once your brain registers that your declaration is your new identity, it will figure out different ways and attract more resources to make it happen.

Re-Wire Your Nerves by NASA

NASA had done an experiment that required astronauts to wear convex goggles 24 hours a day, even while asleep. These goggles flipped everything 180 degrees. The astronauts saw everything in reverse. At the beginning, the extreme stress was obvious. It was reflected in the astronauts' blood pressure. The astronauts then gradually adapted to seeing things in reverse.

21 days after the experiment began, an astronaut, who continuously wore the goggles, was able to see everything normal around him. He still wore the goggles which had not been changed since he first wore them. Over the next several days, other astronauts started seeing everything normal.

In repeated trials, the researchers discovered that the re-wiring did not work if the goggles were removed even for short times.

This summarises that it took about 21 to 30 days of uninterrupted constant input for the brain to accept, adjust to the new input and consider it as normal.

Advance Affirmation by Alec Baldwin

The Edge is a good movie that reflects the Advanced Affirmation. It is played by Anthony Hopkins (Charles) and Alec Baldwin (Bob). Their plane is crashed in Alaska so they are out in the wilderness. A huge bear has been stalking them after killing and eating their friend.

Charles says, "I'm going to kill the bear." Bob looks hopeless and says "It won't work. We can't kill the bear. He is ahead of us all the time. He reads our mind. He's stalking us!" Charles repeats, "I'm going to kill the bear." He then repeatedly demands Bob to say it but Bob remains silent. Charles keeps yelling until Bob quietly say, "I'm going to kill the bear." Bob's face still remains hopeless. Charles repeatedly demands Bob to affirm, "I'm going to kill the bear."

Each time Charles asks Bob to say it louder and louder with more emotional intensity. At the end, Bob has a strong conviction and screams on top of his lung, "I'm going to kill the bear." Charles demands him to repeatedly say, "What one man can do, another can do!" Finally, Bob's face and body language suggest that he has more faith and determination to kill the hunter. Then they go off and kill the bear.

Chapter 8
Miraculous Visualisation
Seeing What You Want and Getting What You See

"Imagination is everything.
It is the preview of life's coming attractions."
Albert Einstein

Visualisation is a mental rehearsal of seeing yourself accomplishing your goal in your mind with an incredible amount of emotion intensity and a strong conviction that you have already achieved your goal. See yourself having better health, a more toned body, a deeper relationship, a better career, a more successful business, financial freedom, a more ideal lifestyle or whatever you want in life.

The Benefits of Visualisation

"I believe that visualization is one of
the most powerful means of achieving personal goals."
Harvey Mackay

Peak performers mentally run important events in their mind before the real event. Astronauts visualise things all the time. Donald Trump made his financial courses more interesting by applying the principles immediately to some imaginary projects in his mind. He said it saved him a lot of time when he started because he was already working on it.

Visualisation accelerates the achievement of your goals in five powerful ways:

1. Visualisation taps into your subconscious mind and uses creative imagination to come up with ideas so that you can achieve your goal faster and easier. New ideas will keep pouring in when you wake up or take a shower.
2. Visualisation programs your Reticular Activating System to notice available resources that have always been there but that you did not notice previously.
3. Visualisation attracts to you the resources, people and opportunities you need to achieve your goal.
4. Visualisation helps you achieve more. When you run an event in your mind several times, you spot a missing step or find a better way to improve process before doing it in real life.
5. Visualisation inspires you to commit to your goals. When you see compelling and vivid images of you achieving your goals, you will desire them even more and do more to achieve them.

In this chapter, you are going to learn:
- 6 Steps for the Powerful Visualisation
- 3 Accelerators of Mind Power
- 5 Captivating Tools that Capture Your Mind

6 Steps for the Powerful Visualisation

"Whatever the mind can conceive and believe, it can achieve."
Napoleon Hill

1. **Identify** what you want, not what you do not want. Use the Pyramid of Life™ and the SMARTER Goal™ in chapter 3: Irresistible Life Design to define your goal.
2. **Visualise** yourself as if you have already achieved your goal. Do not limit your imagination due to your current capability or circumstance. Let your imagination go wild.
3. **Experience** the event as if it is happening now. For example, if you are visualising that you are driving your brand new car, move your hands to steer and your feet to accelerate the speed.

4. **Feel** the feelings of already having it. The stronger you feel, the deeper you will convince your subconscious mind to make it come true.
5. **Believe** that it is already yours. The more certain you are about what happens, the more powerfully your brain can find a way to get it.
6. **Act**. When you feed your goal into your mind before going to bed, your mind will work overnight and hand over the plan. Put a pen and a paper next to your bed, the shower and your bag so that you can immediately write down your plan when it is handed over to you.

3 Accelerators of Mind Power

When you repeat the process over and over for a longer period with clearer images, you have a higher chance that it will come true. There are 3 accelerators that turbocharge your visualisation process: vividness, repetition and duration.

1. Vividness

Add more detail through your senses. Visualise a clearer image, add more sounds and generate a deeper feeling. Enhance the image by making the image bigger and brighter with more intense colour. Play it like a 3D panoramic movie and bring it closer to you. See yourself in and out of the movie from different angles.

Enhance the sound by making it louder, nearer and more regular. Add more environmental sounds and hear them from different angles. Add other senses by increasing temperature and pressure from different locations when you touch. Imagine it tasting and smelling stronger and stronger.

For example, if your goal is to own a beachfront house, close your eyes and see yourself walking in the exact dream home. How is it landscaped? What does the exterior look like? As you walk from room to room, what do you see in the bedroom, living room, dining room, kitchen and bathroom? What pictures do you see in the frames?

What do you hear? What do you smell? What food and drink are you having? How does it taste? What do you touch? How do you feel? It is time to go outside, dip your feet in the beautiful blue ocean and listen to the waves. Breathe in the fresh sea air, smell the ocean, feel the cool breeze on your skin, feel the soft white sand under your feet and feel the sun kiss your skin.

2. Repetition

Visualise it at least twice a day but it should not be a chore. It is your treat to experience your dream coming true in your mind before it expands into your reality. The more regularly you visualise, the more strongly your brain is convinced that it is real, and the more easily your brain can come up with the plans. Add more detail each time you visualise. When your brain is convinced that your visualisation is real, it will find a way to make it happen.

3. Duration

It is about the length of time you hold the image of your goal as complete in your mind. Start by holding it for a few seconds and then extending it to a few minutes. The longer you hold the picture, the deeper it goes to your subconscious mind and the quicker your subconscious mind hands over the plan so that you can make it real.

5 Captivating Tools that Capture Your Mind

There are 5 tools that help you visualise better. Different people prefer different tools. Some people use all of them. Try for yourself and decide which one works best for you or combine them.

1. Text
2. Vision Board
3. Vision Video
4. Visualisation
5. Real Material

Tool#1 Text

Here are the steps:
1. Write down your goal by using the Pyramid of Life™ and the SMARTER Goal™ in chapter 3: Irresistible Life Design.
2. Write down what you commit to give in return.
3. Write down your initial plan for carrying out your burning desire. Refer to the guideline from the 5 Steps to Success™ in chapter 5: Essential Actions.
4. Place your statement where you can easily see it in the morning and night.
5. Go into a quiet spot where you will not be disturbed.
6. Shout out loud the written statement of your goal and the service you commit to give.
7. As you read twice a day, see it as complete, feel it and believe that it is already yours.

An example of a statement is,
"By 01st August 2016, I have £100,000 from the most efficient breakthrough service that I passionately empower people to better their lives and eventually live the life of their ultimate dream. I have an absolute faith and a strong conviction that I now see this money before my eyes. I believe I have this money now. I am touching it with my hands. The money is waiting to be transferred to me. I am awaiting a plan by which to accumulate this money. I determine to follow the plan when I receive it. Please guide me."

Tool#2 Vision Board

"The soul cannot think without a picture."
Aristotle

Your brain and mind respond better to visual stimulation. A vision board is a map of your future. The pictures on the board represent your dreams, goals and ideal lifestyle you wish to create. Find pictures that represent the experiences, feelings and possessions you want to attract into your life and put them on your vision board. You can browse pictures from photographs, magazines and internet. It is better if you put yourself into these pictures and write down the date you created this board and sign.

Put your vision board next to your bed, in your office, on your desk or anywhere that you can see it easily every day. The ideal time is when you wake up and before you sleep. See yourself living it, feel it and believe that it is already yours. The thoughts and images that are in your mind during the last 45 minutes before going to sleep are the ones that will replay themselves repeatedly in your subconscious mind throughout the night.

Leave the pictures on the board even though you have achieved it. When you write down the date you accomplished it and leave it on the board, it reminds you that it is possible to attract things into your life. As you continue to grow, your dream continues to expand. Create a new vision board each year.

John Assaraf cut a picture of a house from the Dream Homes Magazine and put it on his vision board which is the vision board. Every day for about two or three minutes, he looked at his goal, looked at the image, closed his eyes and visualised himself having the dream home. He moved 3 times during the 5 years period. One day, he pulled out the vision board from a box. He realises that the house that he is living in is the one on his vision board. He had bought his dream home without knowing it.

Tool#3 Vision Video

You engage more senses while watching a video. Imagine you are looking at a poster of your favourite movie. Now imagine you are watching your favourite movie in your favourite cinema. Can you feel the different between looking at the poster and watching a movie with surround sound?

You generate more emotional intensity by adding inspiring music and real sound to the images. You can also add empowering affirmations in the video to make it more powerful. Make a movie what you want your life to be and watch it every day in the morning and at night. While watching it, feel the feelings of already having it.

Tool#4 Visualisation

Here are 8 steps to help you visualise better:
1. Go into a quiet spot where you will not be disturbed or interrupted.
2. Walk and take deep breaths by inhaling through your nose 4 times in a row and then exhaling through your mouth 4 times in a row for 5 minutes.
3. Dance to your favourite song for a few minute to jumpstart your metabolism.
4. Close your eyes and give thanks to what you have already had for a few minutes.
5. Concentrate on your burning desire without letting other thoughts come into your mind.
6. See yourself as if you have already achieved it, feel it and believe it is already yours.
7. Give thanks and be grateful for what you just experienced in your mind.
8. Celebrate your accomplishment.

What if You Cannot Visualise?

Look at something, close your eyes and describe what you just saw. Congratulations! You just visualised. Another example? Think of Coke! Did you think as a text or an image? You think in images and you think all the time. This means you visualise things all the time without realising it.

To make it easier for you, looking at a picture of your goal. If your goal is to visit the Eiffel Tower, find a picture of the Eiffel Tower from the internet, cut the picture of yourself and put it on top of the tower as if the picture was taken when you were there. Now imagine what you see, hear, smell or touch when you are on top of the tower.

Tool#5 Real Material

A better way to generate the feeling of having it now is to experience it now. Go test drive your favourite car or view your dream home. Feel the joy of having it now while driving your dream car or walking inside your dream home. If your goal is to own a luxury home or travel to a luxury place, go and be in a luxury environment such as the Ritz hotel. Sit in the lobby, close your eyes, visualise your goal and generate the feeling of having it now. When you open your eyes, see yourself in this new luxury environment and believe that it is already yours. The more certain you are, the faster your brain will find a way.

Jack Canfield was making $8,000 a year but he wanted to make $100,000 in a year. He had no idea how to achieve it. He made a $100,000 bill and put it on the ceiling. So the first thing he saw when he woke up was the $100,000 bill. He then closed his eyes and visualised having the $100,000 a year lifestyle.

30 days later while having a shower, he had the $100,000 idea. He had a book that he could sell but he never thought of selling it. He then noticed the National Enquirer which he had not noticed before. Later he was interviewed by the National Enquirer. The article came, the book sales kicked off, and he made $92,327 that year. He then tried for $1,000,000. His publisher gave him that exact amount for the first Chicken Soup for the Soul™ book.

The Combination of Tools

Mix these tools: Text, Vision Board, Vision Video, Visualisation and Real Material. Every morning and every night, read your first goal out loud, look at the image or the video, close your eyes and visualise as if you have already achieved your goal. Continue through the list until you have visualised each goal as complete. Celebrate!

> *"I Am the Proof that You Can Ask the Universe for It" - Jim Carrey*

Jim Carrey is a very inspirational actor. He was not very successful yet when he drove around the city to perform many times a night in different clubs. Before he went home each night, he drove to Mulholland Drive and parked where he could see the lights of Hollywood. He looked at the city below, stretched out his arms, and shouted, "Everyone wants to work with me. I am a really good actor. I have all kinds of great movie offers." He visualized having directors interested in him and people saying that they liked his work.

He visualized himself as if he was already the biggest star in the world. He saw with his mind that the best scripts and offers were handed to him. He felt so good. While driving back home, he thought he had these things but he just did not have hold of them yet.

He wrote himself a 10 million dollar check, dated it Thanksgiving 1995 and added the notation "for acting services rendered". He carried that check with him in his wallet everywhere he went from that day forth. Just before thanksgiving 1995, he discovered that he was about to make 10 million dollars on Dumb and Dumber.

"It Is All in the Mind" - Arnold Schwarzenegger

Arnold Schwarzenegger is a five-time winner of the Mr. Universe title, an award winning actor, and the former governor of California. He is my number one favourite actor. More importantly I believe that he is the top legendary visionary leader and the world's greatest motivator, who represent achieving what seems impossible. He inspires me and other million people to dream big and go after our dreams. His name and his legacy are going to live for the eternity.

I had the privilege to mingle with him about 10 times in 2014. My first interaction with him was when a host picked someone to ask Arnold a question. But Arnold interrupted and insisted that he preferred to listen to me. I was the only person he chose among 1,000 people. People normally shout out a question but he asked me to wait for a microphone, even though I was just 50 centimetres away and was right opposite him.

He usually gave a minute answer, but he took about 10 minutes to enlighten me. Then he walked towards me and shook my hand. I met him later at a private party. He walked towards me and started a conversation. He created magical moments for me. After several meetings with him, I absolutely adore and admire him even more. He is a great achiever who is very friendly.

After meeting with Arnold, I anchor a strong conviction that I am very important and I am worth listening to, no matter how highly successful the audience is. I learnt a great deal about visualising each experience and maximising each moment.

Before he was Mr. Universe, he was a tank driver who was inspired by a cover of the Reg Park magazine. The more he visualised himself standing up on the stage, the more clearly he knew that he must go to the Mr. Universe competition. He left the military base without permission and sneaked out of the country, knowing that he would be jailed for that. He said it was worth it because he won the Mr. Universe title.

He revealed, "The mind is really so incredible. Before I won my first Mr. Universe title, I walked around the tournament like I owned it. I had won it so many times in my mind, the title was already mine. Then when I moved on to the movies I used the same technique. I visualized daily being a successful actor and earning big money. I visualised being the governor of California. I just knew it would happen."

Lifestyle as You Visualise It - Pitima Tongme

I used the combination of text, vision board, vision video and visualisation for different things at different times. I often visualised staying at the world's best luxury resorts and doing incredible things. My friends ended up taking me to my dream places and doing what I dreamed of.

Another example was when I was working in a night club earning a minimum wage of five pounds an hour. While collecting dirty glasses, I visualised working at JPMorgan and living a lifestyle of someone who was earning over fifty thousand pounds a year. A couple months later, JPMorgan offered me an opportunity in the very competitive Elite Graduate Program in Technology for high-calibre people before giving me a promotion. A couple years later, I was living a fifty thousand pounds lifestyle. You live life as you visualise it.

BONUSES: Master Your Brain™ and Maximise Your Success™

If you think you do not have an imagination or you could not imagine things, watch Tony Buzan, Inventor of Mind Mapping, explain that you have been imagining things all the time without knowing it. He also guides you the best way to maximise your imagination and be more creative.

Listen to Greg Johnson, NASA astronaut for 2 Space Missions, explain how critical it is that NASA astronauts have a good imagination, and how imagination helps him plan and execute things better. He shows you an easy and simple way to visualise things to maximise your success.

www.BeTheUnstoppableYou.com/BookVIP

Chapter 9
Ultimate Rehearsal
The Psychology of Living Your Dreams Now

*"Act as if! Act as if you are a wealthy man,
rich already, and then you will surely become rich.
Act as if you have unmatched confidence and then
people will surely have confidence in you.
Act as if you have unmatched experience and then
people will follow your advice.
And act as if you are already a tremendous success,
you will become successful."*
Jordan Belfort

One of the greatest tools for success is to act as if you have already accomplished it. This means thinking, feeling, talking and acting like the person who has already achieved your goal. Acting as if is not faking when you think of it as your preparation to become who you are destined to be. When you are preparing, you are not pretending. You are doing it.

You can achieve your goals easier when you act as if because:
- You spot a missing step or find a better way to improve a process before doing it for real.
- You gain more confidence when you do it for real because you have done it many times before.
- You send a strong command to your subconscious

mind to tap into the most creative part and activate your Reticular Activating System to help you attract and notice things that help you to achieve your goal.

When you achieve your goal, what is your experience going to be like? How are you going to feel? What character belief, trait and habit are you going to have? How are you going to spend your day? How are you going to manage your time and money? What type of clothes are you going to you wear? Who are you going to interact with? How are you going to treat others? How are you going to speak and respond to others?

Why wait when you can start doing these things right now? You may attract what you want. You definitely attract what you are. When you practice as if you have already achieved your goals, you draw right people, circumstances and things that help to make your dream comes true faster and easier.

Getting a Promotion at Work

"Before anything else, preparation is the key to success."
Alexander Graham Bell

You have a higher chance of getting promoted when you demonstrate that you have already been delivering the same or even better results than the person who is currently at that level. It is time to shine and show your true capability.

It is good to have mentors who are already where you want to be so that they can guide you to get to where you want to be faster and easier. Ask them how they do it, why they do things the way they do and how much it contributes to their success.

Model their beliefs, characters, behaviours and habits. Learn their thinking and planning process. Use the strategies and tools they use. Notice the questions they ask. Structure your communication and communicate like them. Response and treat people the way they do.

Shadow their work. Ask if you can do some of their work for them. Show them that you can do it too. Ask them how you can do things better. Have them mentor you to find your blind spots, unleash your full potential and show you how to remove impediments.

One of the reasons I got a promotion at JPMorgan was that I continuously took on my manager's responsibilities, enhanced them and delivered even greater results that created even more success for me, my teams and my organisation. I have to thank to my managers for believing in me, my mentors for bringing out the best in me and my colleagues for supporting me.

A Classic Way to Start Your Career - Stephen Spielberg

Steven Spielberg is an exceptional director. He took a tour at Universal one summer. During a bathroom break, he hid in a stall until everyone got on the bus and left. He spent the whole afternoon wandering around the studio in the sound stages and cutting rooms. At the end of the day, he borrowed Chuck Silvers's phone to call his cousin to pick him up. He told Chuck what he did. Chuck liked him and gave him a three day pass.

He came back with a nice suit, carried a nice briefcase and was friendly with the guard for the next three days. He came back on the fourth day but without the pass. He waved at the guard, Scottie, who let him in. He had been in the lots and hung out with directors, writers, editors and dubbers every day for 2 and half months.

He then found an office that was not being used so he went to a camera store, bought some plastic name titles and put his name in the building directory: Steven Spielberg, Room 23C. He then went to the main switchboard, introduced himself and gave them his extension so he could get calls.

He showed "Amblin", which was a love story at a beach, to executives at Universal. They were impressed and signed Steven, aged 21, for a seven year contract to direct a television show at Universal. That was phenomenal.

The Paradise on Earth

"It is time to start living the life you have imagined."
Henry James

Host a "Come as You will Be" Party and hire people to play the roles of adorable fans, TV presenters and paparazzi. Everyone is encouraged to envision where they want to be in 5 years and come exactly like that. This is the paradise party where all dreams are possible. At the party, everyone gets to experience the life of their dreams.

Make it more realistic by coming in the style that you would be in 5 years. Wear your dream dress and arrive in your dream car which you just hired. Bring your props such as your mocked up awards, your bestselling books, the magazines that you were featured in, large paychecks you received and pictures of your ideal family, house and holiday.

When you arrive at the party, your adorable fans will be screaming your name and asking for your autograph, TV presenters will be interviewing on live cameras, and paparazzi will be taking your photos. At the party, think, talk and act the part. Conceive, believe and feel that it is real.

Use a past sentence when you talk about what you have already achieved in the last 5 years. Talk in a present sentence when you talk about what you are having now. Play full out, experience your dream life now, talk about your accomplishments, generate a tremendous amount of great feelings and celebrate your success with your guests.

This book that you are reading was one of the things that I envisioned when I played "Come As You Will Be". Dreams do come true. You just have to go for it.

BONUSES: Master Your Brain™ and Maximise Your Success™

Watch Tony Buzan, Inventor of Mind Mapping, teach you how acting-as-if helps you become even more successful in life and business. He also reveals an interesting mind trick.

Listen to Greg Johnson, NASA astronaut for 2 Space Missions, about how acting-as-if helps his space mission become even more effective, and how he applies it in his day-to-day life to succeed at the next level.
www.BeTheUnstoppableYou.com/BookVIP

Chapter 10
Alluring Law of Attraction
How to Effortlessly Attract What Your Heart Desires

"What this power is I cannot say; all I know is that it exists and it becomes available only when a man is in that state of mind in which he knows exactly what he wants."
Alexander Graham Bell

Your thought has a frequency and attract other thoughts, just like the frequency of a radio wave. You can listen to radio 100 FM on your FM dial when you tune into radio 100 FM. To attract the same thought, your thought must have the same frequency. You cannot attract a thought with a different frequency. You cannot listen to radio 100 FM when you tune into radio 105.4.

Your brain has neural oscillation which is a repetitive neural activity in your nervous system. Oscillations have frequency, amplitude and phase. The electroencephalograph is used to measure brain waves of different frequencies. The following frequencies suggest that you can connect your thoughts to your subconscious mind through deep meditation:

- Theta (4-8 Hz) connects your imagining and visualising. It stores emotions, sensations and memories. It relates to your subconscious mind. It is strong during meditation and praying.

- Alpha (8-12 Hz) connects your conscious and subconscious. It is strong when you are relaxed.

Releasing and Receiving Thoughts in a More Effective Way

You increase the intensity of your vibration while releasing and receiving thoughts by attaching an intense emotion to your thoughts.

Positive Emotions [To be leaned towards]

- Burning Desire
- Love
- Inspiration
- Happiness
- Fulfillment
- Faith
- Determination
- Passion
- Excitement
- Gratitude

Negative Emotions [To be avoided]

- Fear
- Frustration
- Anger
- Depression
- Greed
- Anxiety
- Inadequacy
- Jealousy
- Regret
- Guilt

Your Life Compass

Your emotion is your life compass. When you have negative emotions, you are not in alignment with your dreams and expectations. These emotions are the ones you should avoid. For example, you are in a job that you do not enjoy. You are often angry with your boss or colleagues because they mistreat you or do not meet your expectations.

The work makes you feel frustrated because you do not enjoy it. The working hours are too long. Whatever it is, the end result is that you are not enjoying working. This is the time you should consider changing your career or your business to be one you really enjoy and have a passion for.

When you have positive emotions, you are in alignment with your dreams and expectations. These emotions are the ones that you lean towards. For example, you have a passion for your business. You cannot wait to wake up and work on something which seem like you are playing, not just working.

Everything meets or even exceeds your expectations. You get along well with your partners and employees. Your company retains more high-value clients and acquires more new clients than you planned for. Your revenue is much more than you forecast. Whatever it is, the end result is that you are extremely happy about your career or your business. You should stick with this or take it to a higher level.

Thoughts Become Things

"A man's life is what his thoughts make of it."
Marcus Aurelius

Whatever you continuously focus on with an intense emotion, you attract. It does not matter if it is a negative or positive thing. When you attach an intense negative emotion to your horrible thought, you will attract bad things, people and circumstances into your life.

For example, you are worried that you are fat. So you want to lose weight. Weight is what you focus on. It does not matter if it is to gain or to lose weight. But when you focus on weight, weight is what you are getting.

You attract great things, people and circumstances when you focus on attaching only an intense positive emotion while releasing your uplifting thought. When you attach an intense emotion to your thoughts, your subconscious mind picks up your thoughts and subconsciously work on them to make them real.

In contrast of the previous example, you achieve a fitter and more toned body by focusing on being fitter, eating healthier and doing more exercise regularly.

You Are the Product of Your Thoughts

"Life is a mirror of your consistent thoughts."
Napoleon Hill

You are what you constantly think about. Your thoughts attract what you continuously think. Your thoughts create your reality. You do what you do, the way you do, with whom you are doing, at a particular time and place because your thoughts direct you. Every time you sit, eat or drink, you previously thought about sitting, eating or drinking.

"If you do what you have always done,
you will get what you have always gotten."
Tony Robbins

You are the product of the thoughts that you have thought, felt, and took an action towards up until now. What you think, feel and do today determine you experience tomorrow. If your current result is not what you expected, change the way you think, feel and do to be in more alignment with what you want to experience in the future.

The Power to Create or Destroy

Your thoughts can empower you or disable you. Here is an example of the power to create. Have you ever had this experience? Before buying something e.g. a car, you did not notice how many there are around you. After you bought that car, you notice it everywhere.

Here is an example of the power to destroy. Have you ever tried to find something and you could not see it? You kept searching for it in the same area but you still could not see it. You asked someone and he said, "It is right in front of you." You kept looking but you still could not find it. So you kept saying, "I cannot see it! I cannot see it!"

Your friend then came to you and pointed at something right in front of your eyes and said, "Here it is." Then you said, "Oh, I looked at it but I could not see it earlier – strange." Why did you not see it earlier? Your subconscious commanded you not to see it. Your thoughts blinded you.

Creating an Extraordinary Relationship

The relationship can be with your partners, parents, children, friends, mentors, business partners, managers and so on. The following example is for your spouse because an intimate relationship is a fundamental of everything. You can adapt the principle to any relationship. It works.

When you focus on faults that another person has, both you and your partner will not be happy. When you focus on imperfections, you find and attract more of them. You begin to argue. If the arguments continue, it can cost your relationship.

For example, if you focus on their fault which is being late and you kept upsetting them, they may come later or not come at all in the future. If you know they will be late, you do not have to arrive early. A better way is to enhance your relationship in a way that they want to be around you all the time.

> *"The person who sends out positive thoughts activates the world around him positively and draws back to him positive results."*
> *Dr. Norman Vincent Peale*

Trade expectation for appreciation. When you focus on appreciating great things that your partner has, you attract more of them. This creates an even more passionate relationship. Write down everything you love about them. Why do you love them in the first place? What are the happiest or most exciting moments that make you smile when you think about them?

Here are examples:
- I love you because you make me happy and make me smile in a unique way.
- I love you because you are sweet and caring. You treat me well and make me feel love.

- I love you because you take great care of me and our kids.
- I love you because you are always with me especially when I need someone.
- I love you because you inspire me, bring out the best in me and support me to become a better person.
- I love you because you call me daily to ask how my day is when you are not around.
- I love you because you are an action person. You deliver what you say you will, not just talk.
- I love you because we have never had an argument. You are the most understanding person.

Schedule time every day to write at least one thing that you are grateful to them for, and write it down in a journal where you often see it. Use an alarm, a reminder or an application on your mobile phone. Write more things down too when you are thankful for them outside your schedule.

People do more of what they are appreciated for. If you want them to do more of what you want, look them in the eye and tell them every day from your heart what you love about them, what you appreciate them for, feel it deeply in your heart and say it sincerely with love and passion. When you say it from your heart, your partner's heart listens. It is more about their ways of receiving your love, appreciation and connection, not just your way of expressing to them.

For example, approach your partner with a huge smile on your face, look into his eyes and say, "Michael, thank you for your sweetness and kindness. I love you." When they do something special like taking you out for a nice dinner, giving you a big bunch of flowers or taking you for a holiday, say thank you and tell them that you recognise their effort, appreciate them and love them even more. You can make it better by giving them a huge hug, an unbelievable kiss or unforgettable sex.

If you cannot find a reason why you love them, thank them for being them and keep finding the answers why you fell in love with them in the first place. Trust yourself that when you ask why you love them, your answers comes up easily. If you knew why you loved them, what your answers would be.

Apart from trading expectation for appreciation, take 100% responsibility with 0% expectation in return. Find out what their needs are and what drives them. Fulfil those needs and give them more of what drives them. People stay in a relationship and make it even more delightful when all their needs are met. Find out about their needs by thinking of examples or situations that they value the most and figure out the common things about them. Or simply ask them what they value most and what makes them happy.

Then do it at least one thing that makes them feel special and happy every day. Do it for a few months until you notice the difference in quality of a more passionate relationship. Continue doing this and make it your new habit. Be happy, feel love and give love. Make sure your needs are met too.

The Color Purple - Oprah Winfrey

"The way you think creates reality for yourself.
You can change your own reality based on the way you think."
Oprah Winfrey

Oprah read the book "The Color Purple". She was obsessed with it and thought about it all the time. One day she received a call about an audition for the Color Purple. She went to the audition but she did not get a call back for months. She wanted to play Sofia so badly.

While she was praying and crying to God to help her let it go, Steven Spielberg called and said that he wanted to see her in his office the next day. She then understood she drew the Color Purple into her life. She did not know Steven Spielberg. She did not know Quincy Jones who saw her on A.M. Chicago and said to himself that Oprah was to be Sofia.

Attracting Tony Robbins - Pitima Tongme

I had a burning desire to meet Tony Robbins, my role model. A friend told me that Tony was coming to an event in London. During my journey to the event, I focused my thought on meeting Tony with an intense burning desire. I visualised the experience of talking to him and telling him how much he had improved my life.

There were thousands of people attending the event. During an exercise, Tony surprisingly ran down from the stage and immediately lifted me up. He swung me around, gave me kisses on my cheek and looked at me while I was still in the air.

I was shocked. I did not know what to do for a couple of minutes. We finally exchanged kisses on the cheek and then Tony put me down. I was the only lucky person that did an exercise with Tony. I had a chance to talk to him and take pictures with him after the event. My first experience with Tony was incredibly unbelievable.

A couple months later, I went to a gala that President Bill Clinton attended. I did not expect to see Tony but he was there, and he recognised me. After a great conversation with him, he knelt down to take a picture with me. Then he gave me his contact details before I left. He is phenomenal.

> *"I admit thoughts influence the body."*
> Albert Einstein

A Magnificent Power of Self-Healing - Pitima Tongme

One of the greatest compliments that Arnold Schwarzenegger gave me about health and fitness was, "You are in GREAT shape!"

An example of self-healing was during a winter. I had a running nose and sneezed all the time even though I took medicine. A tablet made me felt very sleepy all day. A nasal spray hurt my nose and throat. I used about 50 tissue sheets daily.

It had been like this for almost a month until I tried a new thing -- attracting excellent health. I no longer looked for new medicine. I focused my thought on having great health.

All day long, I kept saying, "Thank you for my good health. Thank you that I am healthy." I felt deeply grateful for having an excellent health already.

When I was about to sneeze, I interrupted my pattern by laughing instead. Then I said, "I am so happy. I have excellent health!" My colleagues thought I was completely mental. My manager asked if I needed a day off to cure my mental health in a funny and cheerful way.

As I declared and expected, I did not have a running nose nor sneeze the next day. I no longer had the fever even though I had not taken any medicine. My thoughts and feeling cured me.

BONUS: Master Your Brain™

Watch Tony Buzan, Inventor of Mind Mapping, tell you the secrets of how you attract people, circumstances and things into your life.
www.BeTheUnstoppableYou.com/BookVIP

PART FOUR

THE ART

OF

FULFILLMENT

Chapter 11
Breathtaking View of Your World
2 Models for the Happiest You

*"In the end, it is not the years in your life that count.
It is the life in your years."*
Abraham Lincoln

Many people are not happy on a regular basis. Many successful people experience frustration, instead of fulfillment. Success does not necessarily mean fulfillment but, when you are more fulfilled, you create even more success.

Fulfillment is a choice. When something happens, you have a choice to experience pain or pleasure. If you are frustrated and unhappy about it, how badly would it affect all areas of your life in the next hours or even an entire day? If you are happy, how wonderfully would your life unfold, and how much more could you achieve?

You switch from frustration to fulfillment by using a simple shift through your model of the world. You use this model all the time to evaluate what things mean to you and decide how you should respond. Your model creates your life experience.

You are going to learn your model of the world through the **Fulfillment Mastery™** and **Fulfillment Catalysts™**, so that you experience a better life with a greater sense of joy, happiness and fulfillment no matter if you are living your dream life or you are in the progress of achieving your dreams.

Fulfillment Mastery™

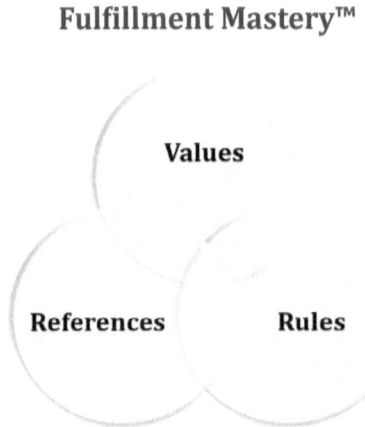

Fulfillment Mastery™ has 3 components: values, rules and references. These components shape your experience and the quality of your life all the time. When you master them, you experience more joy, happiness and fulfillment.

1. Values

"It is not hard to make decisions when
you know what your values are."
Roy Disney

Life values are the things that are most important to you and give you the ultimate sense of fulfillment. Life values are love, happiness, freedom, wealth, success, etc. Your values come from your experience and the conditions that are influenced by your parents, teachers, managers, friends, colleagues and society. But now, life values are something you choose and they come from your own inner voice about what you treasure most. We have an idea about what our values are but we sometimes fear to face what they really are. When we are free from fear and are true to ourselves, identifying life values is easy.

You discover your values by asking the following questions. What is most important to you? What do you stand for? What gives you the deepest sense of life fulfillment? What energises you the most? What are you inspired about most? What have you always most excelled at?

Observe your behaviour. What do you often think about? What you do spend most time on, doing something that you love and enjoy? What do you spend most of your money on? What kind of things will you always find time and money for, no matter what? What topics do you most read, research, listen or watch? What do you often talk about with friends?

Your decisions, actions and experiences are shaped by your prioritised values. When you know the priority of your values, making a decision is easy. There are two types of values: painful values and pleasurable values.

Painful Values

Painful values are things that you are avoiding because they bring negative emotions and experiences. Imagine that your friends gave you a voucher to go skydiving with them. You are on the edge of the airplane. The wind is heavily blowing your face. You hear a loud engine. When you look down, you see the cloud. You are far above the ground.

If your number one painful value is fear and you associate height with fear, you are not going to jump. However, you believe that your friends are going to reject you if you do not jump. If you value rejection more than fear, you are going to jump to avoid rejection.

List your top 3 painful values in the order of what you would do most to avoid. They can be rejection, loneliness, failure, feeling inadequate or frustration. It is not other people's values. It is not something you should, could or must do. List your own values.

Your Top Painful Values

1. _____
2. _____
3. _____

Pleasurable Values

Pleasurable values are things that you are looking forward to experience because they bring you the ultimate happiness and give you the deepest sense of fulfillment.

Imagine that you are offered the most senior position at work but you have you move to another country. Going abroad means that you have to leave your family, who cannot come with you. You believe that the higher position means success and family means love.

Instead of spending days thinking about what you should do, use your core values to decide in an instant. If your number one value is love, you are going to decline the offer and stay here with your family. But if you value success more than love, you are going to accept the offer and go abroad.

List your top 3 pleasurable values in the order of their importance. They can be love, happiness, freedom, growth, success, accomplishment, wealth, contribution or good health. It is not other people's values. It is not something you should, could or must do. List your own values.

Your Top Pleasurable Values

1. _____
2. _____
3. _____

Take a moment to look at your life right now and recognise that you are where you are today because your core values shape your life.

Clearing Conflicting

If you are not where you want to be right now, it is because you have conflicting values that sabotage you. People do more to avoid pain rather than to gain pleasure. If your number one pleasurable value is "success" and your number one painful value is "failure", this conflict prevents you from feeling fully fulfilled. You will not be as successful if you are not willing to fail.

If you have conflicting values, bring them into alignment. If your values are "having more success" and "avoiding failure," change from "avoiding failure" to "having more courage," "having further education," "focusing on prize," etc.

My conflicting values were "success" and "rejection". I was conditioned that rejection means humiliation. I love negotiation. I realise that I must risk rejection if I want to succeed in negotiation. I asked myself, "What could be the worst thing if I ask?" My answer was that people would say no and I would not have the deal that I wanted. I then thought that if I did not ask, the default answer would be "no" and I would not have my deal anyway. My next question was, "What could be the best thing if I ask?" My answer was that I could get what I want. So why not ask?

I recognised that many people had done great deals and I knew that I could do that too. I then realised the truth. Negotiating is a win-win experience. I win the deal or win a lesson. My life has dramatically improved since I changed from "rejection" to "growth". I now love having amazing deals which are sometimes beyond what I thought was possible.

Your Final Values

Your values have shaped who you are today and they continue to shape your future. Look at the above values and ask yourself:

- What do my values need to be to help me achieve my ultimate goals with the deepest sense of happiness and fulfillment?

- What is the ultimate pain that these values will cost me in the long term?
- What values do I need to remove from my list?
- What is the ultimate pleasure that these values will give me in the long term?
- What values do I need to add to my list?
- Why do I list these values in this order?

Your Final Prioritised Values

1. _____
2. _____
3. _____

You feel more fulfilled when you do whatever it takes to experience your top 3 values every day.

2. Rules

*"Rules are intended to provide
a thinking man with a frame of reference."*
Carl Von Clausewitz

Rules are the things that have to happen in order for you to feel great about your experience. Rules define whether your experience is a painful or pleasurable one. When you are happy, your experience meets your expectation as it should be.

What has to happen in order for you to feel love? Does someone need to tell you that they love you every day? Does someone have to hug you, kiss you and want to make love to you? If so, you are on a fast track to unhappiness because your rules depend on something that you cannot control. If you want to experience more love, change your rule to be that you feel love anytime you tap into the overwhelming love that you have for yourself and others.

Changing your rules does not mean lowering your standards on what you cannot control. It is raising your standards to enjoy life at its fullest despite of what happens so that you appreciate life even more. You have within you everything that creates happiness and fulfillment in your life.

A Messy Desk or a Messy Mind

A girl went to her father's desk. "Daddy, your desk is always so messy." He looked at his desk which he believed was tidy. "Sweetheart, can you show me what tidy looks like?" She started moving things around for few minutes. "There you go, Daddy. Now, it's tidy."

He moved a ruler a centimetre down. "No, Daddy! Now it looks messy again. It needs to go back." He moved it back before moving a rubber from the top right to bottom right. "No, Daddy! Now it looks messy again. It needs to go back." He moved it back to its original location before he switched the positions of a pen and a pencil. "No, Daddy! Now it looks messy again. It needs to go back."

He asked what needs to be done to keep it tidy. She said, "Everything needs to be in the exact position that I just put and nothing is moved." He asked, "What if I slightly move something as neatly as I can and let other 15 items remain on their current locations?" She answered, "No. Everything must remain in its position. Otherwise, it will be messy again."

He replied, "It is not about the desk that is so messy so easily. It is that you have so many ways that it can be messy but only one way it can be tidy."

How can you relate this to your life? How many ways that you can feel not so good and how many ways that you can feel great? Sometime we create too many rules to feel bad but only a few rules to feel happy.

> "People are just happy as they make up their minds to be."
> Abraham Lincoln

Here is the guideline for the rules. They should:
- Be simple and easy for you to meet
- Only depend on what you can control
- Have no way for you to feel bad
- Have many ways for you to feel great

Here are a few examples of values and rules against them.

Value #1: Growth

Rule #1: I am growing anytime I learn something new; anytime I do something new; or anytime I stretch myself beyond my comfort zone.

Value #2: Love

Rule #2: I am loved anytime when I tap into an overwhelming love for myself; anytime I think of a romantic moment; or anytime I give love to others.

Value #3: Happiness

Rule #3: I am happy anytime I smile; anytime I laugh for no reason; or anytime I remember something good.

Value #4: Health

Rule #4: I am healthy anytime I stand above the ground; anytime I take a deep breath; anytime I drink a glass of water; anytime I eat healthily; or anytime I exercise.

Value #5: Wealth

Rule #5: I am wealthy anytime I receive money, a salary, a bonus or a pay raise; anytime I find money in my wallet; or anytime I give to homeless.

Values and Rules Alignments

Top Values	Empowering Rules
1	
2	
3	

A Slight Change for a Major Impact

When you are upset with someone, it is because your rules are not met. They may not say or not do something within your rules, or they may say or do something that breaks your rules.

Imagine your rule is that, "If you love me, we talk until everything is worked out. If you walk away, it means you do not love me." Your partner's rule is that, "If you love me, you should not complain about me or my mistakes. If you complain, it means you do not love me and I should walk away." When you have an argument with your partner and point out what they did wrong, they will walk away. They think that you do not love them and you think that they do not love you.

You have a choice to clearly communicate and compromise. When you know each other's rules, offer what you are willing to do to make them feel happier. Say, "I am happy not to point out what you did wrong. Instead, I will say that I am going to appreciate you even more if you do a different thing that meets my rule. Is this acceptable to you?" Once you have agreed what you are willing to do, ask what they are willing to do to make you feel even more love and not walk away.

People may forget about rules. Be understandable and tell them what you appreciate them for and remind them nicely what the compromised rules are. I know a couple who agreed on rules while they were dating. These agreed-upon rules are non-negotiable no matter what. They framed them and put them in their bedroom. They said they have been happily married for over 20 years because of the rules.

3. References

"Nothing has a meaning except for the meaning we give it, and since we are making up a story anyway, we might as well make up a story that supports us."
Harv Eker

References are your beliefs that have been shaped by your experience. They are the things that you have seen, heard or experienced. Your references help you interpret what things mean, how you feel and how you should respond. In regard to your dancing style, for example, what is the difference between identifying yourself as a crap dancer and the next Michael Jackson?

There are 2 kinds of references: unique references and global references. Unique references are for a particular thing. Global references are for everything. Imagine that your boyfriend was not nice. Your unique reference was that your boyfriend was not nice. Your global reference was that men are not nice. What a massive difference can these references have on your next relationship?

Your state determines what reference you are going to use. Imagine below.

You are watching a horror movie called A Nightmare on Elm Street. Freddy, who wears his razors gloves, just killed someone. He is now chasing another victim. You are in an anxious state or a scary one. A door behind you suddenly opens. Your cat makes a loud "meow" noise and moves toward you very fast. What would be your first reaction? I would be nervous for the first few seconds.

What if you are watching Tom and Jerry instead? Jerry just kicked Tom's body and ran away. Tom is chasing Jerry. Tom suddenly steps on a banana leaf that Jerry put on the floor as a trap. Tom makes a funny "meow" sound and slips through a door. At the same time, your cat, which looks just like Tom, makes the same noise and moves toward you at the same pace. What would be your first feeling and response this time? I would be laughing for the first few seconds before I got up and checked on him.

Using Contrast to Appreciate Life Even More

Imagine that you stay in a 4 star hotel. The first scenario is that you are bored and think that this is not a very nice hotel. You then look outside your window on your left and see a dirty hostel. You probably think that you are very lucky and have a better perception of your hotel.

The second scenario is that you are very happy that you stay in this grand hotel. You go out to your balcony, look on your right and see a 5 star resort which you like even more than your hotel. You are highly inspired by its beauty. You probably want to upgrade and stay in that resort. How can the same hotel make you feel differently? It is because of a comparison.

Use contrast to create an alternative feeling and perspective. No matter how bad you think things are in your life, look outside the window and notice that someone has it worse. If you prefer not to take their place, be grateful for what you have and acknowledge how lucky you are.

In contrast, no matter how well you think things are in life, look outside the window and notice that someone has it better. When you think you reach the top, look at a different view and discover that there is a higher level.

Have you seen a Nike Commercial, level 7 Success at Success? Richard Branson told Kobe about his achievements and then said, "I feel like I am already living success at success. I am just wondering what is left." Kobe said, "Richard Branson, you have achieved success at success. But have you achieved success at success at success." Richard answered, "No, I have not." Kobe encouraged, "You can do better. I know you can."

Your Best Day in Disguise

"That which does not kill us makes us stronger."
Friedrich Nietzsche

Your worst day is your best day in terms of lessons you choose to learn from, and the growth you choose to experience. Think about the achievement that you are most proud of. During the progress of achieving it, had it been the easiest or hardest journey? You were at your best just after you were at your worst because you made a massive breakthrough and became a much better person.

The most challenging thing in life is the biggest opportunity, which you will remember for years. It could be a divorce, a life-threatening illness or getting fired from your job. You may not see any positive things at the time. When you look back, however, you will be thankful for it. Why wait for a month or a year when you can embrace it and appreciate it right now? You create your feeling, not your circumstances.

A divorce gives you an opportunity to stay away from who is not right for you so that you make room for the right one. A life-threatening illness allows you to examine yourself, remove a habit that does not serve you and create more empowering habits. Being made redundant makes you revaluate yourself and gives you an opportunity to find a better job or even start up your own business. I am not suggesting that you should get a divorce, have a serious illness or get fired. I am saying that you can use your reference to turn everything into a good thing.

A Different View that Changes Lives - Steve Jobs

During his speech at Stanford University, Steve Jobs said he was publicly fired at the age of 30 from Apple, which is the company that he founded. He did not know what to do for months. He thought about running away from the valley.

By using contrast, it helped him better interpret what getting fired from Apple really meant. He found that the heaviness of being successful was replaced by the lightness of being a beginner again. It freed him to enter one of the most creative periods of his life. He soon realised that getting fired from Apple was the best thing that ever could have happened to him.

When he used a different reference to change the way he looked at things, the things he looked at changed. And so did his response. His new response to the same experience led to a better life. Instead of running away, he found NeXT which is also known as Pixar. Pixar created the world's first computer animated feature film, Toy Story, and is now the most successful animation studio in the world. He also fell in love with an amazing woman who later became his wife. He was sure none of this would have happened if he did not get fired from Apple. At the end, Apple wanted him back to create products that change lives.

Expand Your Reference, Expand Your Life

The key is to expand your references to support you to achieve your dream faster and easier. Having more references helps you better evaluate what things mean so that you respond better. There are lots of ways to expand your references. Here are few examples:

- Experience something new.
- Read biographies of people who are already where you want to go, learn how they get there and model their success.
- Attend seminars that help you achieve your goals.
- Connect with new people who are where you want to be and learn from them.
- Watch inspiring true-story movies to learn from them.
- Go skydiving to experience having more courage.
- Race a super car at a professional circuit to experience more excitement.
- Travel abroad to experience new culture.
- Donate to a shelter to experience the joy of giving.

Fulfillment Catalysts™

*"The only way to live is to
accept each minute as an unrepeatable miracle,
which is exactly what it is, a miracle and unrepeatable."
Margaret Storm Jameson*

Fulfillment Catalysts™ help you experience a greater sense of joy, happiness and fulfillment whether you are living the life of your dreams or you are in the progress of achieving them. It contains 3 activities.

1. Grow
2. Give
3. Be Grateful

Fulfillment Catalyst #1 Grow

"Without continual growth and progress, such words as improvement, achievement and success have no meaning."
Benjamin Franklin

Achieving things is not going to keep you happy. No matter how hard you have worked to achieve your goal, you are going to ask, "Is that it?" You have seen many high achievers who live the life of people's dreams but they are not happy. They reached their peak and they stopped growing. They have little or nothing to look forward to. I was one of them until I changed. Life fulfillment comes from your journey and your progress. Every living thing must grow. If you are not growing, you are slowly dying inside.

There are many ways that keep you learning and growing:
- Have your next goals lined up so that you have something to look forward to.
- Develop a higher standard and live it every day.
- Continue learning, improving and be the best you can possibly be.

- Try new things, go to new places and meet new people.
- Find a team that challenges you at the next level.

Take a moment now and write down at least 3 things that you are going to do to keep growing.

_____
_____
_____

It is great to keep track of your achievements. I ask people who come to my events to spend a few minutes writing down their achievements. If you were there with me, you would notice that their physiology changes while they are writing. They smile and say they are happier. Take a moment now and write down your top 3 greatest achievements to date.

_____
_____
_____

It is good to find a journal or diary, write your previous achievements in the dates prior to today's date and then write down your achievement for each day. A good time to write is in the evening so that there is time to accomplish something if you think you have not accomplished anything that day. You can also achieve more things too.

Fulfillment Catalyst #2 Give

*"We make a living by what we get.
We make a life by what we give."*
                    Winston Churchill

We all have a deep desire to contribute beyond ourselves and our responsibilities. Your deepest sense of fulfillment comes when you sincerely and selflessly help, give, share and support others. Everything has to contribute or it will be eliminated. The great way to give is to leave your legacy beyond your life.

There are many ways that you can contribute even more:
- Put a smile on someone's face to share joy and happiness.
- Leave your legacy that will improve the quality of people's lives.
- Give your time and knowledge by mentoring someone or giving talks at events.
- Talk to a homeless person, make them feel loved and buy them something of their choice.
- Join a charity or give something to a charity.

Fulfillment Catalyst #3 Be Grateful

*"We can only be said to be alive in the moments
when our hearts are conscious of our treasures."*
Thornton Wilder

You are more fulfilled when you trade expectation for appreciation. Gratitude gives you a better perspective of life that allows you to see more miracles around you. It reminds you of the good things in your life. It turns a bad thing into a good thing and a good thing into a great thing. It trains your brain to focus on what you truly want on a consistent basis.

*"At times our own light goes out and is rekindled by a spark
from another person. Each of us has cause to think deep
gratitude of those who have lighted the flames within us."*
Albert Schweitzer

There are many ways that you can feel more grateful.
1. Have a gratitude diary
2. Give thanks to others
3. Do a gratitude session

Gratitude Diary

It can be the same diary in which you write about your achievements. Write down who or what you are grateful to, and what for, on each day. Do it daily. It can simply be "I am grateful to .... for ...."

Gratitude Giving

People feel good when they are appreciated for who they are and what they do. It is important to thank them and let them know that they impacted you in a special way. This does not only make them feel good but it also makes you feel great.

Visit them to give them genuine thanks, tell them what you appreciate them for, let them know what a difference they made in your life and mean it. If you cannot visit them; call them, text them, email them or send them a thank you card.

Gratitude Session

You will be more fulfilled when you do this exercise for 5 - 15 minutes every morning when you wake up and every night before you go to sleep. Here are the steps.
1. Take a walk.
2. Take a deep breath. Inhale through your nose 4 times. Exhale through your mouth 4 times. Do this for few minutes before breathing as normal.

3. Think about everyone you appreciate. Start by thinking about yourself, your parents, your spouse, your kids, your friends, your mentors, your business partners, your teams and everyone else you are grateful for.
4. Think about ideas, strategies, tools, opportunities, challenges and anything else you are grateful for.
5. Think about what you are grateful to them for.
6. Say out loud who or what you are grateful to and what for.
7. See the events replayed in your mind.
8. Feel that you are blessed and know how lucky you are.
9. Think of your next goals. See it as if it had been done perfectly. Feel your achievements and give thanks to everyone and everything that helped make your dreams come true.

Below are examples of what you can be grateful for:
- Your achievements.
- Their love and support.
- Their encouragement and inspiration.
- Their time and attention.
- Their belief and faith in you.
- Their presence during challenging times.
- Special treats that they gave you.
- Joy and happiness that they brought into your life.
- Your dream that they made come true.
- The best things that they saw or brought out in you.
- Opportunities and challenges that they gave you.
- Challenges that they helped you to overcome.

My Story

Karate Kid, Legally Blonde and Facing the Giant Within are the movies I used to watch when I required massive courage to accomplish what seemed impossible. More recently, I watched my own movie to build an unshakable confidence that I could achieve anything I decided to. Now, I have an absolute conviction with my whole heart that nothing is impossible. If you want to be more confident, I encourage you to create your movie. Check out an example video at www.youtube.com/watch?v=m11ZDHLivbk

You are going to know my three unstoppable dreams, the rise of the unstoppable me and my commitment to the unstoppable love. This section is added as a suggestion from my good friend, Tony Buzan, Inventor of Mind Mapping. I am an ordinary person, just like you. Perhaps you can relate to these stories.

An Ordinary Person with Extra-Ordinary Dreams Going Extra Miles

From Zero to Million in 2 Years

When I was twenty three, I aimed to have a million bahts before I was twenty five. It was a very ambitious goal for someone who was almost homeless. During my free trip to Japan as the university presentative for my university, I noticed that the exchange rate between Thai bahts and UK pounds was 70 to 1. So I decided to work in the UK.

When I arrived in London, I did not know anyone. I came with little money. My English was poor. I did not know the culture. People took an advantage of me. More importantly, the university did not accept me because my English was poor.

I expanded my comfort zone as an introvert to be more comfortable as an extrovert. I never cook, wash my clothes or iron but I had to sacrifice this luxury to live my bigger dream. I practiced cooking, washing, ironing and cleaning. Most of the time the food was burnt. My clothes often got holes in them while I was ironing.

Even I could not understand my English. Before people understood me, I had to say the same thing in different ways many times. I could not understand others either. So I studied English to communicate better and to re-take the IELTS exam.

A couple of months later, I had more friends. My food became better. There were no more holes in my clothes. My English was better. I passed the IELTS. I was accepted by Brunel University where I graduated with a Master's degree.

After graduation, I applied for major investment banks but I had no job offers no matter how many job applications I sent out. However, I got an offer from the Guardian Media Group. A few months later, I applied for JPMorgan, got accepted in the very competitive Elite Graduate Program in Technology for high-calibre people and got promoted.

I made my first million baths before I was twenty five. Why work harder in Bangkok, with no hope of becoming a millionaire, when I could work smarter by taking an advantage of the exchange rate? I planned to go back to Bangkok after my first million baths but my dream was expanded.

Life Changing Decision

I fell in love with the UK. I wanted to make the UK my new home. I found out about the Highly Skilled Migrant Program visa, HSMP, which would allow me to work in the UK longer.

The challenge was that I had to earn 12 months' salary within 9 months because I started working late. I found out about this visa 4 months before my visa would expire. I had only 4 months left to earn that much salary on my payslip. My family and friends told me it was impossible. They consistently asked me to go back to Thailand.

I am a determined person. I did whatever it took to increase the amount of money on my payslip. I asked for a pay raise, worked on remote sites to claim expenses and had a night job. I woke up at 7 AM, worked and slept at 3 AM.

To make it even more challenging, I was heartbroken from the first guy I ever loved. I was often chased by gangsters in a dark alley when I finished work after midnight. I was challenged both physically, emotionally and mentally for a few months. At the end, I got the HSMP visa. I am happy that I am now a British citizen.

The Unstoppable Book

I told people that I wanted to write this book. My family, friends and mentors consistently discouraged me. Everyone told me that I would waste my time and it would not work. The top three things they often said to me were:

1. I was no one.
   When they said this, I giggled and asked if they forgot my name. I then playfully recommended them to learn from my memory champion friend.
2. I achieved nothing.
   They knew I was penniless and almost homeless many times. They also knew that more recently, I made my first million bahts before I was 25 and I just became a British citizen a few months ago.
3. There was no market for self-development.
   They heard about Tony Robbins and his success.

I ignored the naysayers and wrote this book anyway. People saw me carrying the manuscript around and asked if they could read it. They fell in love with the manuscript. They even paid me before this book was published. The naysayers become my clients. My friends become my raving fans.

I want to emphasise that your voice is the only voice that matters when it comes to your destiny. If you lose your voice or let those who speak on your behalf compromise your voice, your dream will be lost forever.

As you do not drown yourself, do not drown your voice. Your voice matters. Trust in your voice. Believe in yourself. Go get your dreams. Do not stop until you get it. Make the most out of this book.

The Rise of the Unstoppable Me

Fear Is Not Danger

When I was seven, my mother dropped me off at a musical school. After school, I phoned my mother to pick me up. She told me to take a bus. I had never took a bus. I did not know which bus to take, where to get on, how to get on, how to pay, how to get off and where to get off.

I was scared but it did not stop me. I asked people questions until I got on a bus. I often passed my stop and walked back to where I wanted to go. This taught me that feeling scared did not mean I was in real danger and the best way to deal with fear was to go through it until I mastered it.

Against the Bullies

A boy bullied and hurt me when I was seven. I told my mother. She commanded me to fight him the next day or I would face her. The next day I was involved in a bad fight with the boy who was much bigger than I was. I had cuts and bruises but those were the last ones.

Since I stood up for myself, the boy and other people never bullied me again. I am not suggesting that violence is the best way to fight against bullying. I am just saying in my case, I was glad that it worked.

Silence Drown

I could not swim. I always almost drowned when I was in a river, a lake or the sea. Every time I was drowning, no one helped me even though there were at least two people with me every time.

I had to trace back my steps and most of the time climbed up to a higher level to escape the drowning. That experience did not stop me from playing in the water. I knew if I almost drowned, I could always survive when I refused to give up.

My Commitment to the Unstoppable Love

The Power of Love

I love my mother. She always came home at 4 PM but she was late one day. It was after 5 PM and she had not arrived yet. Someone once told me that the Goddess was powerful. When we wished, she made it come true. But the price I had to pay was that I could no longer eat beef.

I went to the Goddess and prayed for my mother. I said if my mother came home unharmed within the next fifteen minutes, I would no longer eat beef for the rest of my life. She came home unharmed within that period.

People told me it was a joke about not eating beef. My mother told me to eat beef. But I always keep my words. Even though beef was my number one favourite, I never ate beef again since I was seven.

From Pain to Power

I witnessed a heart-breaking experience. I love dogs. My little sausage dog was not well so I attended to it. My neighbours who were older boys came into my house with a fishing net. They picked my little dog up and put him in the fishing net. Then they bounced him on the ground and laughed out loud.

I tried to rescue my beloved dog but they grabbed me and hurt me too. After a couple bounces on concrete, my little dog bled. They took him out and went away. I attended my dog and took the very best care of him until he died a few days later. I swore that day to protect dogs.

I had a lots of scars from protecting animals. For example, I saw a man about to throw a heavy metal stick to a puppy who entered into his shop. He was too far. I could not stop him in time so I ran in front of the puppy and kicked the metal away. But I miscalculated where I should kick. The metal had a spike. It hit me deep. I was injured badly. My mother asked if it was worth it. I said it was. With the size of the metal and the spike, the puppy would not stand a chance. To me, it was only a scar. To the puppy, it would have cost his life.

Great Gift of Giving

I always contribute to those who are less fortunate, especially people on the street or kids in a shelter. When I was in Bangkok, I always bought food for a shelter, played with the kids, gave them toys and made them feel love.

In London, I always talked to people on the street, took them to their favourite fast food restaurants and bought them whatever they wanted. In winter, I bought winter clothes and gave to them. I also raised money for charities.

5% of the profits from this book goes to Centre Point to give homeless young people a future. Be part of our team and help people just because you can.

You Can Change the World

The essence of transformation is not just about you. It is about the entire world. If you want the world to be a better place, start with you being better. It is your duty to grow yourself to your fullest potential so that you create the greatest abundance of success and happiness in your life.

All of us who have the capacity must remember that we have the responsibility to give something back. Your contributions makes a difference in other people's lives and makes this world a better place. To better the world, you must first better yourself and then start changing someone else's world, one by one. Giving has a ripple effect. It will come back to you.

I ask you to commit to help those less fortunate enjoy a greater quality of life with more success and happiness. A simply way to do this is to share this life-transformational book with many people as possible.

Commit to telling at least one hundred of your friends, family, business partners, colleagues, neighbours and others about this book, *Unstoppable You*™. Give them this book as a life-changing gift.

Your journey is a true blessing when you have your family and friends share this extraordinary experience with you. You help each other create even more success and happiness.

My dream is to make the world a better place by unleashing human potential and improving the quality of people's lives. I am fascinated by your desire to expand your life. Together, we change the world for the better. I therefore ask you to kindly help me make this dream a reality. Share this book with the world!

I am powered by your success. Spread your happiness and share your success stories that can better someone's life, or even the world, at www.BeTheUnstoppableYou.com/Contact

GOOD NEWS

To help you achieve even more, purchase the following amazing materials at www.BeTheUnstoppableYou.com

Additional Material	Value
Success Map™: the Ultimate Map to Your Dream Life	FREE
Maximise Your Success™ By Greg Johnson, NASA Astronaut for two space missions	£50
Master Your Brain™ to Get What You Want By Tony Buzan, Inventor of Mind Mapping	£50
30 Minutes Coaching Upon the Purchase of "3 Hours Private VIP Coaching"	£150

Special Offer for Celebrating
the Author's 10 Anniversary in the UK.
This Offer Is Valid until December 2015.

Total £250

BETTER NEWS

Congratulations for buying this life-transformational book. I want to invest in you. You can have the above materials for **FREE!!!** Claim your rewards at
www.BeTheUnstoppableYou.com/BookVIP

Success Map™

Success Map™ is the ultimate map to your dream life. It is the most important model that completes the jigsaw puzzle in this book. Everything you learn from the Formula of Achievement is neatly and completely glued here.

Success Map™ powerfully projects your life goal and the perfect path to achieve your goal. It empowers you to use both your left and right brain to strongly signal a powerful message to both your conscious and subconscious to realise your goal and make it reality.

Maximise Your Success™

It is an opportunity not to be missed, to learn from my dear friend, Greg Johnson, the Superior Performance Award Winning NASA Astronaut and the President of CASIS.

Greg reveals significant strategies on how to succeed at the next level. He communicates the perfect blend of powerful strategies, breathtaking stories and compelling examples that you can easily understand and relate to. The way he conveys his message can capture your heart in an enjoyable and exciting way. You can achieve what seems impossible after listening to this extraordinary wisdom and applying what you learn.

Master Your Brain™

What if you can unlock more brain power to achieve mega success in every area of your life? An ancient computer took men to the moon. Your brain is more powerful than that computer. Imagine what more you can achieve when you maximise your brain power.

Tony Buzan is my dear friend who invented Mind Mapping and found the World Memory Championships. He has written over 140 books which have been translated in over 39 languages about how to make best use of your brain.

In this video series, Tony and I reveal the most fascinating yet simplest step-by-step system to maximise your brain and memory to get whatever you want.

Your data will be vividly well organised so that you can easily access it. Once you master this skill, you will never forget anything you have heard, read or seen. Your creativity and imagination will be dramatically improved.

You are going to see more possibilities and become limitless. You are going to change the way you think, feel and behave to instantly become more successful. You are going to be amazed at how much more you can accomplish and how much better your life can be. Start now!

Your Success Journey with Pitima Tongme

*If a man can land on the moon,
you can certainly land on your dreams.
Pitima will show you how.*

Private VIP Coaching

The Ultimate Way to Getting the Life You Want

What do the TOP 1% Highly Successful People have in common? A Coach! Private Coaching is a MUST! This is for those committed to living life at a level few ever attain.

This is an unforgettable life-transforming experience to work one-on-one with Pitima personally to focus on solving your specific challenge or designing the life you truly desire on your own terms. We then create powerful plans that empower you achieve your biggest goal with incredible success and lasting fulfillment.

You will discover the drivers of your thoughts, emotions, actions and habits before aligning your beliefs, values and rules that pull you towards the direction of your ultimate dreams. You will achieve your biggest dream faster and easier.

You will uncover the hidden patterns that stop you from reaching your full potential, and the unrealised triggers that motivate you and make you unstoppable. You will tap into your full potential, unleash unconscious resources and bring out the best in you.

At the end of the session, you will have a clear compelling vision, a step-by-step action plan and a strong conviction that you can accomplish anything. You challenges can be resolved. Your goal can be achieved.

Keynote Speaking

Pitima delivers the perfect blend of highly-valued life-changing strategies that are packed with actionable results-oriented content, heartfelt inspiring stories that incredibly move your emotions and inspire actions, compelling examples that you can relate to and step-by-step plans to help you achieve greater success and fulfillment.

Pitima speaks from the heart with passion, compassion and confidence in a charismatic, authentic and enjoyable way that quickly and deeply connects with you and inspires you to take action.

Pitima brings the wow experience that engages your audience in a special way and makes them feel great about themselves and your event.

Corporate Training

Now, more than ever, your organisation's success is hugely derived from the performance of your people. Pitima has over half a decade's experience in empowering CEOs, Directors of Fortune 100 Companies, Managers and Employees overcome challenges so that they can achieve their biggest goals faster and easier than they ever thought possible.

Pitima tailors trainings to address your corporation's unique needs and is able to provide specific solutions to achieve your most important objectives. The trainings range from one hour talks to full day programs. The most demanded topics are:

- The SMARTER Goal™ for Unlocking Your Full Potential
- Time Mastery System™ for Doubling Your Productivity
- Negotiation for Reducing Cost and Increasing Revenue
- Strategic Thinking for Being Unstoppable
- Better Attitude for Retaining Clients for Life

Success Academy™

Skyrocket Your Success at Your Best

Success Academy™ is a life-transforming experience of getting ultimate results for high achievers. This is where extraordinary people meet.

You may have extraordinarily accomplished more than most even dream of doing in their lifetimes, but deep down in your heart you know there is another level that you have yet to attain.

Pitima reserves this programme for truly exceptional people who are not settling for less than what they are capable of being, doing, having and giving. When you complete this program, the year ahead is going to be your best year ever.

About the Author

Pitima Tongme is the UK's leading life coach and the CEO of Success Mastery. She is committed to help you achieve your biggest goals faster and easier than you ever imagined.

She consistently delivers breakthrough results through outstanding products, world class events and executive coaching throughout America, Asia and Europe. She is living proof of her life-transforming strategies which are proven by the success of her clients and herself.

She is trained by the best trainers such as Tony Robbins. She cares about you and your success. She can open more doors for you by connecting you with her multi-millionaire friends and the best-in-class experts from all walks of life.

Whether your intention is to overcome a challenge or achieve a goal, her focus is to help you get the result that you want.

www.BeTheUnstoppableYou.com

www.ingramcontent.com/pod-product-compliance
Lightning Source LLC
Chambersburg PA
CBHW022003160426
43197CB00007B/252